JOHN PAUL RUSS' the
MONSTER
HUNTERS'
SURVIVAL GUIDE

zenescope
WWW.ZENESCOPE.COM

WRITTEN BY
JOHN PAUL RUSS

ILLUSTRATIONS BY
SHAWN MCCAULEY
ANTHONY SPAY

INKS BY
ANDREW MANGUM

TRADE DESIGN BY
CHRISTOPHER COTE

EDITED BY
RALPH TEDESCO

**THIS VOLUME REPRINTS THE
SERIES THE MONSTER HUNTERS'
SURVIVAL GUIDE ISSUES #1-5**

WWW.ZENESCOPE.COM

FIRST EDITION, JULY 2011
ISBN: 978-0-9827507-8-0

ZENESCOPE ENTERTAINMENT, INC

JOE BRUSHA - PRESIDENT
RALPH TEDESCO - V.P./ EDITOR-IN-CHIEF
ANTHONY SPAY - ART DIRECTOR
RAVEN GREGORY - EXECUTIVE EDITOR
CHRISTOPHER COTE - PRODUCTION MANAGER

JOHN PAUL RUSS' the MONSTER HUNTERS' SURVIVAL GUIDE

TABLE OF CONTENTS

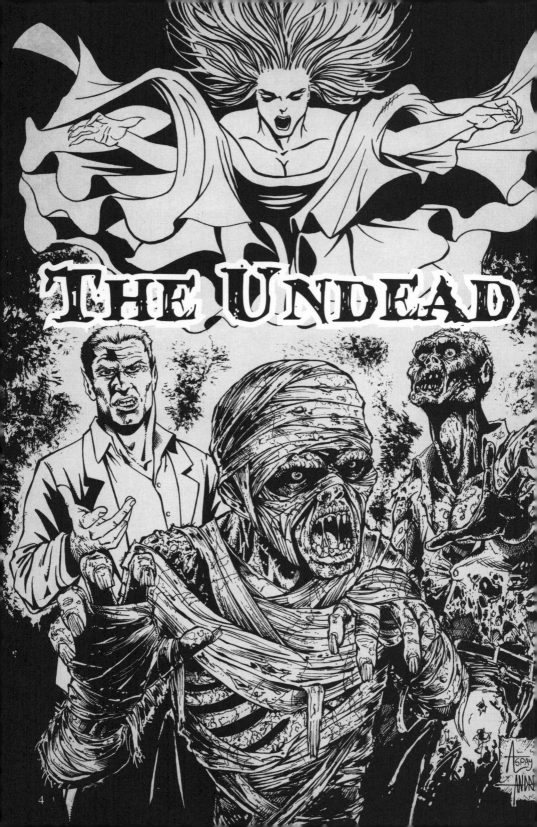

Introduction to Monster Hunting

For as long as humankind has inhabited the Earth we have fought against things that go bump in the night. As children we are told that the sights and sounds that haunt us are simply nightmares, our imaginations run amuck. But not all shadows in the darkness that force us to call out for our mommies and daddies can be so easily explained away. The soothing words that help us fall back into slumber also fail to prepare us for the true dangers in the world.

Monsters are real. They have been with us throughout history and even before. They are responsible for countless deaths, killing us one-by-one or wiping out entire civilizations with the swipe of a claw. Those of us who answer the call to defend our brethren against these vicious beasts carry on a rich tradition that can be traced back centuries. We are the unsung heroes of the modern era.

We are the Monster Hunters.

Monster Hunting is a calling.

The decision to join the ranks of Monster Hunters should not be made lightly. The training is intense, the hours unending, and the danger is very, very real. Too many alcohol-fueled frat boys have been torn to shreds under the foolish belief that it would be fun to go into the woods to find out if Werewolf rumors are true.

Today's Monster Hunter does not lead a glamorous life. We are not held in regard like our predecessors, the ancient heroes of world mythology. Quite the opposite. It is in our best interest to keep Monster Hunting a clandestine activity to avoid widespread panic among the populace. We live cut off from our loved ones so they remain safe. We have contacts, not friends. Bases of operations, not homes.

In spite of this lonely existence, I have found that Monster Hunting is one of the most rewarding of callings available to mere mortals. But it is not a lucrative career. In spite of my many successes, I certainly have not gotten rich killing Monsters. But the undertaking does have its rewards. At the end of a hard day of fighting—or a month long siege—I can rest secure in the knowledge that evil has been destroyed, lives have been saved, and the world as we know it continues to exist. Society holds our pro athletes and actors up as heroes while Monster Hunters are mocked and ridiculed. I personally have saved the earth from destruction on more than one occasion…you tell me who is more important to society.

It's been said that Monster Hunting was born in that moment when the first cave man killed the first dinosaur. And yes, I know "caveman" and dinosaurs did not live at the same time, but that's not the point. As humans, we are relatively young on the planet. Monsters pre-date us. Evil has been around since before we crawled out of the primordial ooze. That is the reality of the challenge we accept. The battle for this planet is monumental and unending.

Before the advent of modern travel technology, the random Vampire Hunter or Zombie Killer focused on a specific form of evil. When travel took weeks or months it was pretty unlikely that these hunters would encounter more than one or two kinds of Monsters. Knowing how to fight Sea Creatures was worthless for a person that never saw the ocean.

Now that we can travel the world in a matter of hours, it is only logical to be prepared in all areas of Monster Combat. It takes rigorous training to ply this craft. Only the strong survive. The rest die horrible, gruesome deaths. Trust me. I know.

The best recruits are often chosen at a young age, sought out by older Monster Hunters who mentor the apprentice until they are skilled enough to go out on their own. It is strongly suggested that, unlike the ill-advised frat boy in the earlier example, anyone wishing to pursue the art of Monster Hunting seek out the advice of an expert before entering the field. But even years of training may not be enough to prepare them for battle. I have lost too many apprentices because they insisted that they were ready in spite of my objections.

With that in mind, I have devised The Monster Hunters' Survival Guide as a basic primer on some of the most vicious boogeyman that haunt our reality. Along with important information on their varied origins, this book also lays out the facts necessary to identify these beasts and the most effective methods to fight, capture and kill them. Within these pages, I have compiled the key components every Monster Hunter will need to not only thrive in this calling, but ultimately to survive.

Monsters were here before us. They won't be here after us

"Monster" is a generic term that describes all manner of creature no matter their origin or intent. It is important to understand that not all Monsters are created equal. They have a wide variety of abilities, strengths, and weaknesses. Some are powerful enemies, while others can be nullified without even breaking a sweat. Some possess intelligence and can be as cunning as the smartest human. Some have supernatural abilities that make hand-to-hand combat nearly impossible.

Another crucial fact is that not all Monsters are necessarily evil. Some, like Sasquatch, are for the most part docile in nature (although even they can be dangerous if provoked), others look like hideous freaks of nature but pose no threat to humans. Some of those that are evil, like Vampires, are indistinguishable from normal humans to the untrained eye. This distinction makes the job of the Monster Hunter all the more important in a society that is ready to attack anything perceived as different. We must know when it is proper to raise our weapons and when to back away.[1] Used properly, this guide will help you determine the most dangerous of Monsters as well as the safest, most effective way to deal with them.

When combating those monsters that are evil, the best weapon a Hunter can possess is knowledge. But this is not limited to the comprehension of whether a chainsaw or a flame-thrower is the best instrument to use against a Zombie.[2] A true understanding of a Monster's history and motivations will present important clues for dealing with the enemy.

No one knows exactly when the first recorded Monster attack occurred. Ancient civilizations are filled with supernatural tales of Gods and Monsters, but it is unclear which of those stories are fact and which are merely tales created by fertile minds. What we do know is that evidence of unusual beings has been found in every country on the planet and in every point in recorded history.

---

1. When in doubt, I say raise the weapon.
2. Chainsaw

As for the origin of individual Monster species I have divided them into three main categories: natural, supernatural, and scientific. These groupings cover a broad spectrum of rational explanations on the existence of Monsters. In some situations, the cause of these Monsters can straddle more than one form of origin. Zombies, for instance, were once creatures of magical, or supernatural, origin, but a new breed of walking dead can be attributed directly to a scientific fiasco.

Natural Monsters are those that have been born out of some isolated trait in human or animal development. A rogue chromosome or a unique strand of DNA exerts itself, giving birth to a being with no precedent. Oftentimes these Monsters are merely a little known species that is simply misunderstood, like the Sasquatch. But in some cases, their status as an evolutionary anomaly impacts their personality turning them into vicious bastards.

Supernatural Monsters are somewhat harder to define since there are many different explanations for their existence. Their origins are debated on par with the questions regarding God and the Devil. This I do know: there is magic in this world. I've seen it. I've used it. But controlling it is hard as hell for the average mortal Monster Hunter.

The Scientific cause of Monsters needs no explanation. These wretched devils are the result of man's egotistical inability to accept his place in the universe. One would think Mary Shelley's fictional masterpiece Frankenstein would have been enough of a warning to stop messing around with the natural order of things. Your average "politically correct" scientific defenders will argue that creatures developed through this research have helped in dealing with the problems of man. But those same advocates are the first to pee their pants and run when confronted by one of the Zombies they let loose on the world.

You must first learn to walk before you can disembowel

The three tenets of the Monster Hunter are: **Identify, Contain, Neutralize.**

The reason we go by the name Monster Hunter instead of Monster Killer is because we understand that the Hunt is the most important part of our work. The first rule in any good Hunt is to identify the problem. Know the creature's motivations, its strengths, and its weaknesses. Only engage once you've learned all that there is to know about your prey.

Containing the Monster is another key point in any Hunt. Don't go rushing into the fight. First lock down the area. This is not just to protect the innocent victims in the vicinity, but for your own protection as well. Always watch your back. There is no need to risk a sneak attack from possible cohorts. Only engage once the threat is contained

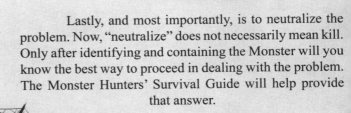

Lastly, and most importantly, is to neutralize the problem. Now, "neutralize" does not necessarily mean kill. Only after identifying and containing the Monster will you know the best way to proceed in dealing with the problem. The Monster Hunters' Survival Guide will help provide that answer.

All right, now. Enough with the introduction. It's time to get into the essentials. Your quest for knowledge on the road to becoming a Monster Hunter starts with perhaps the most dangerous of all the monster categories…The Undead.

Various factions of Monster Hunters use different symbols to identify their guild.

VAMPIRE

Origin: Natural
Locale: Major cities,
Small towns, suburbs &
occasionally rural areas
Identifying traits:
Pale skin. Fangs
Effective Weaponry:
Stake to the heart
Ineffective Weaponry:
Religious Icons
Best Time to Hunt:
Daylight hours
Worst Time to Hunt:
Following a feeding
Threat Level: High

An immortal being that feeds off the blood of the living, possesses increased strength and agility, and procreates through a blood exchange with its human victims.

There's a lot of life in the Undead.

Vampires are one of the most famous—if not the most famous—Monsters of all time. To be clear, they are Monsters, not simply misunderstood, tortured anti-heroes or any of the other lies the public has been fed by books and movies. It's important to separate fact from fiction before going into the field under the belief that a clove of garlic will stop a Vampire from ripping out your throat.

For most of history, Vampires were seen as demonic, soulless creatures embracing their hunger for blood. Evidence of Vampiric beings has appeared in almost all civilizations. They have gone by many names, including Lamia, Strix, Lilu, Langsuyar Fifollet, and Vampyr. Whether or not these are the true forebears of the modern Vampire is unclear, but the stories surrounding most of these demons fit the basic profile of a Monster that drains life from its victims.

The term "Vampire" entered mainstream usage during the European Vampire Outbreak of the 18th and 19th centuries. Numerous Vampire accounts were published during this time, including the quintessential history of the Vampire in *Bram Stoker's Dracula*.[3] The story centered on the former man believed to be the progenitor of the modern Vampire, the 15th Century Prince of Wallachi, Vlad Tepes, better known as Vlad the Impaler.

Today, you may encounter the lone Vampire in your travels, but these bloodsuckers are social by nature. They have developed a loosely knit societal structure of covens all around the world. These covens are not united under any one leader. There is no ruling council that sets up a uniform system of laws for them to follow. Loosely maintained pacts keep the peace between covens, but they are entirely dependent on the volatile nature of the beings that entered into them. As a result, the covens are often at war with one another as these creatures are aggressive by nature and have a biological imperative to assert their dominance. An intelligent Monster Hunter can use this hostility to his benefit, turning the Vampires against one another to let them fight it out for him.

It is commonly believed that these modern Vampires are descendants of Vlad Tepes and part of his "bloodline." But his progeny are not the soulless demons of campfire stories. Research has proven that Vampirism can be explained as a horrifying mutation of human genetics that can be passed on through an intentional infection of its victims.

3   Unlike Shelley's fictional Frankenstein, Dracula is based on true, though greatly exaggerated reports.

Vampires are immortal. You are not.

All Vampires were once human, but their humanity died along with their bodies. The immortal being that is resurrected may show traces of the original personality, but the new biological imperative toward feeding overwhelms all reason, making even the most gentle Vampire a killer when the thirst sets in.

A Vampire is created when a human is drained of blood to the point of death. The infecting Vampire can either complete the murder or stop feeding before the heart stops beating, leaving the victim weakened, but alive. A third option is to give the victim a generous portion of the blood now coursing through the Vampire's veins. This will pass along the virus that activates a genetic mutation in the victim's body. The virus kills the victim and brings it back as an immortal entity with above average strength and agility, a nearly invincible body, and an unnatural hunger for blood.

Unlike Zombies or Mummies, Vampires can blend with the human populace with only minimal camouflage. A notable pallor to the skin (except immediately following a feeding) and fangs are the primary visible signs that they are different from humans, but the observant Monster Hunter knows there are much more telling clues.

Being dead, or Undead, Vampires do not breathe or have a heartbeat. They do not eat or drink anything other than blood. Their skin is cooler to the touch and extreme temperatures do not affect them in the same way as humans.

The upper canine fangs are retractile and only come out in feeding mode, which is another reason it is difficult to distinguish them from humans. Most Vampires can control the revealing of their fangs, but when the thirst is upon them their teeth will extend involuntarily.

Vampire saliva contains a mild paralytic sedative that incapacitates the victim once bitten to avoid a struggle. It can also erase all memory of the attack. A small dose of the Vampire's advanced healing powers can also be passed through the saliva, as most bites heal over quickly with only minimal scarring. A trained Monster Hunter can easily distinguish the small double puckering of the skin that denotes a bite, where the average person would find only a pair of blemishes.

Much has been made over the centuries about the Vampire "thrall;" the alleged hypnotic and/or telepathic abilities these Undead beings possess. Through extensive interaction with Vampires, I've determined that this idea is a lie, probably originating from the long-lived nature of these creatures. They have studied our behavior over decades and centuries and probably have a better insight into human nature. This allows them to use their charisma to persuade victims into behaving in a previously unimaginable manner. Training and experience have given me the skill to resist a Vampire's charms, but I have witnessed many a helpless victim happily follow a Blood Sucker to death after a simple flirtation.

As they only come out after the sun has set, Vampires have evolved to have acute night vision. They are also experts at using the shadows to camouflage themselves, which combined with their increased speed, explains their ability to seemingly disappear in the wink of an eye. These traits are also possible explanations for the disproven myths that Vampires were able to fly or turn into mist or animals when more superstitious minds were looking for a reason to explain their sudden vanishing act.

Vampires are among the most challenging Monsters to hunt. Not because of the things that make them different from humans, but for the one thing we both share: Intellect. Unlike Zombies or Werewolves under a full moon, Vampires possess the same level of intelligence they had before death. Older Vampires have the additional benefit of years of collected knowledge far superior to what one human can learn in a lifetime. This makes fighting them not only a physical challenge, but a mental one.

Of course, their physical attributes are nothing to be taken lightly. Vampires have very few weaknesses. The supernaturally fast healing abilities also make them a dangerous foe, often able to outlast Hunters that fail to deal a killing blow early in a confrontation. The longest single battle I have ever had with a Vampire lasted an entire night. By the end of it, I suffered several broken bones and a partially severed ear. The Vampire was dead. Though they are immortal beings, they are definitely killable. It just requires the proper training.

Vampires lie dormant during the day because of an extreme sensitivity to the ultraviolet rays of the sun. This should make the daylight hours a prime time for Hunting Vampires, except that most compensate for this vulnerability by making sure they are well protected while resting.[4]

Sunlight itself is a rather ineffective weapon as it can take hours to kill the Vampire depending on the strength of the creature. (By the same token, consuming a Vampire in fire is also effective, but slow.) There have been some strides in the development of technology that can focus ultraviolet light as a weapon, but we are still years away from that as a practical solution.

Religious iconography has no effect on the modern Vampire at all. Crosses and holy water are weapons of the past, trading on the creature's own superstitious belief in its creation. We suspect that it was only through the powers of suggestion when Vampires believed that were truly soulless demons, that their own fear rendered these weapons powerful.

The primary weapon in a Monster Hunter's arsenal when taking on a Vampire is the wooden stake. The short, carved daggers can be made from any wood, but ash and hawthorn are the traditional choice. This is largely due to a holdover of beliefs in the protective nature of these trees from when Vampires were thought to be demonic. It helps to carry a mallet to pound the stake into the heart if you are not strong enough to complete the task on your own. In that case, however, I'd say that Vampires are not the best adversary to approach at this stage in your Monster Hunting career.

Decapitation, preferably with a sharp silver blade[5], is another effective means for dispatching a Vampire, although it is not a permanent solution. The Vampire's advanced powers of regeneration will allow for the head to reattach itself to the body if not properly disposed. The primary method to destroy a Vampire corpse is to burn it and scatter the ashes in different locations. If time is a factor, then the head and the body need to at least be buried in two separate locations.

---

4   If you do decide to take on a Vampire in its sleep, watch out for guards or defensive traps.
5   Silver was initially believed effective against Vampires because of it being a "pure" metal, but modern science recognizes that it has more to do with the high electrical and thermal conductivity of silver that affects these creatures.

Everything you think you know about Vampires is wrong.

That is to say everything you know outside of this document is wrong. There are many myths out there about Vampires that can get you killed. The fertile minds of fiction writers more interested in making a buck then recounting a true history of these fascinating creatures has produced an incredible amount of disinformation about these deadly monsters . I have been able to debunk the following myths in my encounters with Vampires. Commit this list to memory as it may save your life one day.

- Crosses, holy water, and other religious icons have no ill effect on Vampires, but they may slow the older, more superstitious ones down temporarily.

- Garlic is also useless. I mean, really. Garlic?

- Vampires do not need to sleep in soil from their homeland. The traditionalists still do prefer coffins to beds, although there is no reason they cannot sleep in a bed if the room is sufficiently protected from daylight.

- Their images do reflect in mirrors and they can be captured on film. I have the photos in my files to prove it.

- They are able to cross running water, however they do need to be invited into a private residence in order to cross the threshold.

- They are not shapeshifters. Vampires cannot turn into animals, however most animals are sensitive to these creatures and avoid them at all costs. The notable exceptions are rats, bats, snakes, and spiders, which are drawn to them.

- Vampires do not sparkle. If you see some pale person getting all sparkly in the sunlight, do not kill him. It's just an emo kid wearing body glitter.

Psychic Vampires

Similar to their namesake, Psychic Vampires consume the life force of their victims, though they drain energy and emotion as opposed to blood. They are often incorrectly catalogued with Vampires as "Undead" due to this similarity, but they are living humans with supernatural abilities.[6]

Tales of these individuals stretch back through history in various cultures, but the term "Psychic Vampire" (also "Psy-Vamp") only gained popular awareness in the mid-20th century. It is generally used to describe a condition wherein spiritually or emotionally weak people drain energy from others to build up their own. This is a natural affliction that can be fought with basic emotional focusing techniques. Often, the Psychic Vampire is not even consciously aware of his or her effect on others.

In rare cases, a person with this affliction can learn to intentionally focus it on others, becoming an energy predator that feeds on humans and nature. At times, they will not stop until their victims are either dead or an empty shell of their former selves. Monster Hunters should approach with caution as they do not need to be in physical contact to use their power.

In preparation for an encounter with a Psychic Vampire, Monster Hunters need to build up their spiritual energy. This can easily be managed through yoga and meditation. Strong energy fields are a natural deterrent to Psychic Vampires as they often prey on the weak. Suppressed memories and emotions are a magnet to these parasites, so don't come to battle with any unresolved issues that can be used against you.

Energy shields, including protective amulets made from crystals—particularly the quartz crystal—are useful charms in defending against attack. You can also strengthen your own auric field through focusing techniques as simple as envisioning a bubble of white light surrounding you. To assist those already under attack, you can extend your aura to strengthen theirs but you need to be in  physical contact. This, however, may weaken you in the process, so you must calculate the necessity for this action in your dealings with the Psychic Vampire.

The most effective manner of defeating this enemy is to overwhelm the Psy-Vamp with positive emotion. True, it's not as dramatic as staking a traditional Vampire or decapitating a Zombie, but it is a proven technique. Focus your own positive thoughts in the direction of the enemy until he is weakened to the point that it is safe to take him into custody. As Psychic Vampires are human, it is difficult to kill them without raising questions from local law enforcement, but containment procedures do exist to neutralize their abilities.

6   In spite of their humanity, we include Psychic Vampires in the section on the Undead since most readers will seek them out here.

Incubus & Succubus

The Incubus and Succubus are two sides of the same coin, male and female demons in human guise that use their seductive energy to steal the life force from mortals during intercourse. Repeated sexual contact with these demons will weaken the body, sometimes to the point of death. Succubi and Incubi are wrongly confused with Vampires in the way they have their own thrall-like charisma to entice their victims and take their life force, but they are not the Undead.[7]

During more puritanical times, these demons inflicted their evil on unsuspecting victims in their dreams, often leaving their targets unaware that they had come under attack. Today they have created a more seductive dance in order to gain their victim's trust and access to their bed. But make no mistake, even with consent, these demons are murderous evildoers who must be stopped.

7   Like Psychic Vampires, we include the Incubus & Succubus in the Undead section to ease your search for information.

In battling these creatures, the first action is to remove the victim from the situation. This is not always as easy as it sounds. I've dealt with many victims that have grown emotionally attached to their demon lovers and refuse to leave them. The last thing you need is some love-struck guy throwing himself in front of you at a key moment in the battle.

Once the victim is safe, a banishing spell is the best way to destroy the demon. Depending upon the strength of the enemy, these spells can be as simple as standing in the center of a pentacle drawn on the floor and commanding the demon to leave or more complex requiring the use of ritual tools. It is best to prepare the area in advance to avoid the possibility of the demon physically attacking you before the spell can be enacted. I will admit that I have fallen under the charms of a particularly sensual Succubus or two during my career. Of course, that never stopped me from performing my duty once we both got what we wanted out of the encounter.

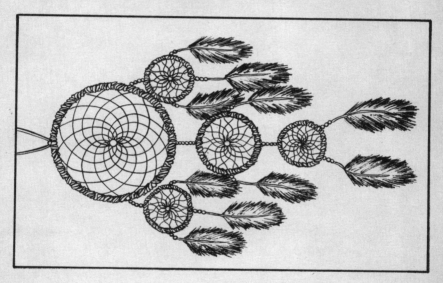

Native American dream catchers hung in the victim's bedroom windows are useful in keeping these demons from returning. They need to be authentic charms constructed properly out of willow and strung with sinew. The cheap replicas sold in gift shops have absolutely no effect on supernatural beings.

MUMMY

Origin: Supernatural
Locale: Egypt (Though not exclusively)
Identifying traits:
Linen wrapping
Effective Weaponry:
Magic
Ineffective Weaponry:
Traditional hand weapons
Threat Level: High

A corpse that has been embalmed to preserve the flesh and has now reanimated through mystical means, most often associated with the Ancient Egyptian civilization.

The intentional mummification of a corpse through embalming was a prevalent death ritual in many societies throughout history. Likewise, stories of these mummified remains—or Mummies—rising from the dead crosses numerous civilizations, though it is predominately associated with Ancient Egyptian culture. For our purposes, I will focus mainly on the Egyptian Mummy as they have the highest number of recorded resurrections of this admittedly rare phenomenon.

Ancient Egyptians believed that a person's soul left the corpse upon death and was doomed to wander the afterlife if it could not reunite with the body following burial. Of the five components of the Egyptian soul, this specifically related to a reunification with the Ka (the vital energy of life) and the Ba (the person's character). For this rejoining to occur, the body needed to be well preserved to survive the journey into the afterlife.

As part of the preservation process the organs—except the heart—were permanently removed and placed in canopic jars. The flesh was anointed with oils and perfumes and treated with natron or other preservative minerals. The body was then wrapped in hundreds of feet of linen bandages for protection and laid to rest in a sarcophagus surrounded by sacred charms for mystical protection.

The two most integral points in the burial ritual for the Monster Hunter to understand are the recitation of prayers over the deceased and the weighing of the heart. A priest intending to help the voyage to the next world would recite prayers from The Egyptian Book of the Dead, a collection of over 200 spells for the deceased. Though these spells were designed for protection, it is now believed that, in some cases, darker incantations were used for nefarious reasons.

The weighing of the heart was also a key moment in the journey as it was believed that the soul resided in that organ. Anubis, The God of the Dead, would decide that if the heart weighed more than the feather of Maat (the Egyptian concept of truth and balance) the deceased behaved well on earth and deserved eternal life.

Most causes of Mummy attacks can be traced back to the spells performed by the priest during the death ritual intended to either protect the corpse and its treasures or to curse the dead. Egyptian Pharaohs were laid to rest in grand tombs and buried with treasures that made them tempting for grave robbers. Statues of Anubis would guard their tombs while curses were often inscribed on the walls and doorways. In some cases, bricks were placed at the four corners of the tomb, each with a spell from the Book of the Dead inscribed on the surface. Most reported cases of Mummy attacks have come following an interloper breaking into the tomb and making off with the treasures.

In some cases, the Pharaohs themselves have been cursed to walk the Earth as punishment for their deeds in life. This makes the Mummy a victim in its own way as well. The flipside of this are the Pharaohs that sought to cheat death and live an eternal life straddling both worlds. In either of these cases, the cause of their reawakening can be traced back to the ritual of their death. Mummies that have been punished are easier to dispatch as it merely relies upon an undoing of the spell that trapped them in their current state. That basic premise is the same for those who intentionally returned, though that is often more difficult because they do not wish to go so willingly.

Not all Mummies are found in tombs.

Up to this point, we've been looking at mummification through a controlled exposure to chemicals. However, other causes of mummification can be found in nature. Well-preserved corpses have been discovered in extreme cold or dry conditions and saline or acidic water. The "bog body" phenomenon of corpses that have retained their skin and internal organs is responsible for over a thousand bodies dating back to the Iron Age found in the wetlands of Northern European countries.

Some of these bodies have been killed in a ritualistic manner, often as pagan sacrifices in a less enlightened time. Like the Mummy of Ancient Egypt, understanding the ritual is key to determining the combat techniques in the rare case that one of these "Natural Mummies" is brought back to life. Recorded instances of these types of Undead Mummies are exceedingly rare to the point where I question them to be true at all.

What is more likely a cause of these Natural Mummies returning to life can be found in the section on Zombies. In these cases, the corpse is chosen because it is usually in a better condition than the traditionally buried, decomposing body. It is then reanimated through mystical means as a slave to the spellcaster. To combat this type of zombified Mummy, please refer to the section on Mystical Zombies later in this compendium.

Bog Mummy

Every Mummy has a story. Learn that story and you will know how to defeat your enemy.

Mummies are one of the "big four" in the Monster world along with Vampires, Werewolves, and the fictional Frankenstein.[8] But Mummies are distinctly unique for a number of reasons, which makes their combat more difficult to categorize. Modern cartoons would have us believe that all one needs to do to destroy the Mummy is unwrap the linen bandages to reveal no actual threat inside. Anyone reading this who believes that should put these pages down and go take up needlepoint.

One of the best things about combating these undead creatures is that Mummies, unlike Zombies, Vampires and Werewolves, can't create new versions of themselves. In one case I did encounter a Mummy that had the ability to turn a human victim into a mindless slave, but the hold was severed—and my apprentice returned to me—when the Mummy was destroyed. Either way, they do not have the power to infect others and turn them. This is relatively good news as is means there no such thing as a Mummy Outbreak.

What they can do, however, is use powers similar to a necromancer to waken other dead beings, most often in the form of skeleton warriors. I have never had the luck to witness such an event, but I have read several cases where Undead armies have risen and quickly outnumbered inexperienced Monster Hunters that were taken completely by surprise. The only way to effectively combat these overwhelming forces is to take out the Mummy that has called them back to life. Once that happens, the army generally returns to its resting place, if not just collapsing in a heap where they stand.

8   Though some would say that "Frankenstein" has recently been replaced by Zombies.

Unlike Vampires or Werewolves, there is no agreed upon universal way to kill a Mummy. Being creatures of magic, they are protected by a host of supernatural powers that make them powerful beyond most Monsters. A stake through the heart or a silver bullet will not cut it. Decapitation is useless as well. Oftentimes their skin is too strong to be pierced, but even if you could hack a Mummy into tiny pieces it would always regenerate. Modern weaponry does have an effect on slowing Mummies, but is relatively useless in bringing an end to the threat.

Perhaps no other Monster is more difficult to kill because the Monster Hunter needs to understand the Mummy's motivation before it can be dealt with. Vampires want to drink your blood and Zombies want to eat your brain, but the motivation for a Mummy is different in each case. Even when a Mummy has risen because the tomb was disturbed, the Hunter needs to understand how the tomb was invaded, what if anything was taken, and how to properly to return the stolen goods. You can't just throw a necklace into the tomb and run. There is always some significance to the object's placement.

Researching the specific Mummy's history is a must. In cases where the Mummy was cursed by a priest or was a powerful Pharaoh that sought power beyond life, it is essential to know what method was used to bring the corpse back as the Undead. All spells have a way to be reversed or possess some kind of weakness that can be exploited. Many times, the magic controlling the Mummy is centralized in an amulet worn around its neck. Sometimes simply removing that amulet will end the spell.

In all cases of Mummy reanimation it is essential to consult with a historian familiar with the civilization and the historical period in which the Mummy was

laid to rest. I've found that a basic understanding of Egyptian hieroglyphics is also useful, but you will need to consult with an expert linguist or archeologist familiar with these symbols in order to reverse any spell. Several of my colleagues have met their doom through a misinterpretation of a single word. These are beings of the oldest magic and require proper magic to be dealt with. Hunters who only dabble in magic should leave well enough alone and call in a true expert.

NON-CORPOREAL BEINGS

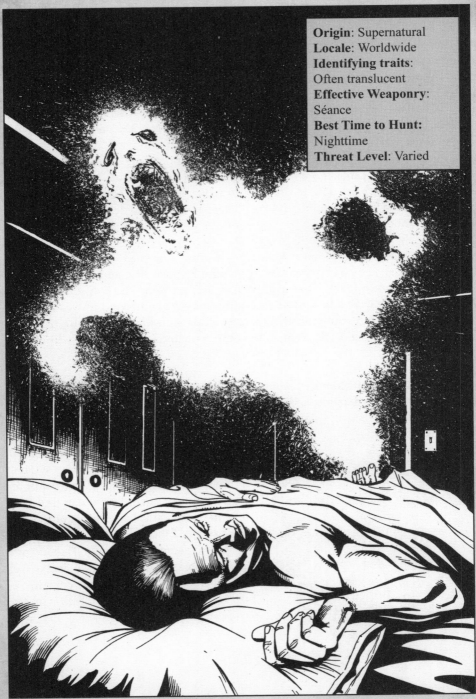

Origin: Supernatural
Locale: Worldwide
Identifying traits:
Often translucent
Effective Weaponry:
Séance
Best Time to Hunt:
Nighttime
Threat Level: Varied

Entities with no true physical form, whether a spirit, soul,
or other manifestation of intangible energy.

Ghosts

Most cultures believe that our souls live on after death, moving onto the after-life or some other plane of existence. As a result, no beings among the Undead are more ingrained in our collective conscious than the souls of the dead that remain bound to earth. They go by many names—such as Phantoms, Spirits, or Specters—but they are mainly known as Ghosts.

The explanations for Ghosts are almost as numerous as the many different world religions. They manifest as either an invisible force affecting people and objects, indistinct ethereal forms, or nearly corporeal beings that only reveal their true identities when they float through the air or walk through walls.

Ghosts are generally bound here due to some type of unfinished business. That means they can't be defeated in the traditional sense using weapons or magic. They must be assisted onto the next phase of the afterlife. By determining what binds them to their previous lives a Monster Hunter can help resolve what was left undone so they can move on. It's all a little "touchy feely" at times, which is why I tend to avoid these Undead spirits and leave them to the people that want to be reality show stars.

From my experience, Ghosts come in two forms: Benevolent or Malevolent. Another way you can categorize the differences between them is those spirits that know they are dead and ghosts that have no idea they have passed on.

Benevolent Spirits usually remain behind out of concern for their loved ones or, in cases of untimely death, they are searching for the reason behind their demise or justice for their murder. These Ghosts are the least of a Monster Hunter's concern, though you can certainly help them find "closure" if you feel inclined. Keep in mind, that just because a spirit starts out as benevolent does not mean it cannot turn evil. Being caught between life and afterlife can be confusing and even the friendliest Ghost may not be aware that its turmoil is causing harm to others.

Malevolent Spirits are usually on a mission. They could simply be angry with someone they left behind and cannot cross over until they cope with the grudge they carried into death. They could have been miserable bastards in life and carried their evil into death where they now have paranormal abilities to lash out at the living. I have my own beliefs about Heaven and Hell, but it's a safe bet the more intensely evil beings refuse to cross the threshold into the afterlife out of a fear of what's waiting there for them. Researching the history of an area for stories of any questionable deaths or murders is a good way to determine the identity of the spirit and the reasons for its behavior.

Ghosts cannot be tracked in the traditional sense. Being non-corporeal, these apparitions can simply disappear and reappear on a whim. Cold spots or an ectoplasmic mist with no rational explanation are often indicators of a ghostly presence. Some people are born with sensitivity to the supernatural while others can hone their "sixth sense" with training. In either case, the following tools are useful in determining the presence of a Ghost:

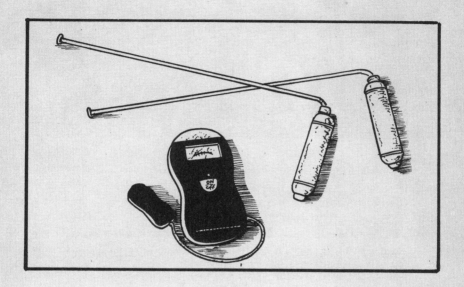

Cameras and Audio Voice Recorders
Some electronic equipment is useful at tracking what the naked eye can miss.

EMF and ELF Meters
Measure disturbances in the electromagnetic field.

Dowsing rods
Forked or straight rods that work in a similar—
though lower tech—manner as an EMF reader.

Thermometers
Either infrared, remote sensor wireless, or hardwired thermometers can pick up sudden changes in temperature that sometimes indicate a ghostly presence.

Infrared Cameras and Motion Sensors
Focusing on this specific wavelength of the visible light spectrum can sometimes reveal otherworldly entities.

Do not call on a Ghost unless you are prepared for it to answer.

A séance is an effective way of communicating with Ghosts to determine what their problem is and how to help them move on to the next life. Many times a Ghost just needs to be heard and the séance itself is enough of an emotional deliverance of any unresolved issues. In some cases, a key piece of information simply has to be relayed to a loved one before the soul can pass.

There are as many ways to conduct a séance as there are different belief systems in the world. They range from an intricate affair led by a Medium with a gathering of loved ones or the more simple use of a Ouija board. Scrying through reflective surfaces or crystal balls are also effective means of communicating with the dead.

A more extreme form of a haunting is a possession in which a soul has entered a living body (or home) and refuses to leave. In that case, an exorcism may be required. This is not something the average Monster Hunter should attempt on his own. Though the concept of exorcism rose to prominence along with Christianity, it is an ancient ritual. The basic idea is to force an invading spiritual essence to swear an oath to leave the victim or building. As these practices differ between religions, you really should contact the head of the local houses of worship to determine the best course of action for the evil you intend to remove. (Of course if the possessed person is dangerous you may have to take matters into your own hands.)

Poltergeist

Poltergeists are a mischievous astral life force that can turn a household upside down. They are behind many of the reported hauntings attributed to Ghosts but they are not spirits of the dead. Nor are they demons, psychically active children, or any of the other urban myths that have been used to explain this rare phenomenon.

Poltergeists do not take a physical form, which makes them impossible to identify through traditional means. They first announce their presence through ominous, unexplained sounds before moving on to physical manifestations. These can include foul odors as well as objects flying through the air, being overturned, or rearranged. Raining stones on their victims is another common occurrence. They can also manipulate electronic equipment, turning lights on and off and interfering with telephone signals.

What I've described may seem like little more than a nuisance, but severe cases of Poltergeist activity are not only emotionally traumatic, they can cause bodily harm and even death. Their victims have reported being slapped, claw marks appearing on their skin, and their bodies being tossed out of bed. In extreme cases victims have reported being sexually assaulted. Though they have no corporeal form, Poltergeists can animate objects, using them to cause harm.

Like Psychic Vampires, Poltergeists are attracted to strong emotions and tend to attach themselves to prepubescent children since these years are filled with emotional turmoil. The astral force feeds off that energy, turning it into a manifestation of their mischief. This has often misled paranormal scientists to claim that the children themselves are the ones causing the mayhem through some form of psychokinesis. This is a lie that is harmful to children already being victimized by the Poltergeist attack.

Poltergeist activity starts suddenly, crescendos in a matter of months and subsides on its own within a year, though I was called in on one case in Miami where the Poltergeist was in residence for a several years. Whether the Poltergeist has been clanging around for weeks or months most victims cannot bear to experience this kind of upheaval in their lives for any amount of time.

Since a Poltergeist usually attaches itself to a family member, simply moving out of the house rarely solves the problem. Sprinkling salt around the home or burning sage are two of the more basic means for removing evil spirits and Poltergeists are no exception. Banishment spells are also useful. In one of my easiest encounters to date, I politely asked a Poltergeist to leave the premises and it complied. But these simple answers are not always the proper solution.

Poltergeists are energy parasites, instilling fear in their victims and then feeding off that fear. The more fear they absorb, the more powerful they become, which allows them to increase the intensity of their attacks. At a certain point, the amount of fear they can elicit from their victims levels off, which is why Poltergeists eventually move on. The best way to force that to occur is to rob the Poltergeist of those strong emotions, which is often easier said than done as it relies on the victims to find their own strength, leaving much of the "combat" out of the hands of the Monster Hunter.

Wraith

Wraiths share many qualities with the other Monsters discussed in these pages. Like the Mystical Zombie we will examine shortly, this ethereal being is under the control of another. It is a mindless slave that carries out whatever it master commands. Similar to the Psychic Vampire and Poltergeist, it feeds off the darker emotions of the living, able to drain them of energy and strength. And like the Malevolent Ghost it is called forth from whatever realm it originates to seek revenge on any enemy, though not its own.

In some ways the Wraith is also a victim. It did not ask to be conjured by whatever powerful spellcaster has forced it to do his bidding. But don't take too much pity on these beings. Wraiths enjoy performing these evil tasks because they gain strength through the misery they brings to others.

Again, like the Psychic Vampire, the best way to fight this ethereal being is through positive emotion. This will not destroy the Wraith, but weaken it enough to give you more time to find the spellcaster pulling its strings. The only way to permanently dispose of a Wraith is to return it from where it came by either reversing the magic that called it up or kill the spellcaster that conjured it.

Banshee

The Banshee is a spirit fettered to a family of Irish or Scottish heritage. Unlike the Poltergeist that also links itself to a family, this supernatural being is not a temporary companion. The Banshee stays with a family from decades to centuries, until the entire line has died out. The Banshee's keening cry can be heard at night announcing the coming death of a member of the family to which she has become attached. A gathering of several Banshees foretells the death of someone of great importance.

Banshees are mistakenly considered evil as their cry is often confused as calling death upon a household, but it is only a portent and not the cause. In its purest form, the Banshee's cry is a gentle warning, meant to ease the living into acceptance of their coming death. But that does not mean there aren't malevolent Banshees. In cases where the Banshee feels nothing but hatred toward the family to which she is fettered, that howl is a shrill celebration of the anticipated demise. There is as yet no known way to unfetter a Banshee from her family.

9   But I am working on some theories that I hope to include
       in future editions of my collected works.

ZOMBIE

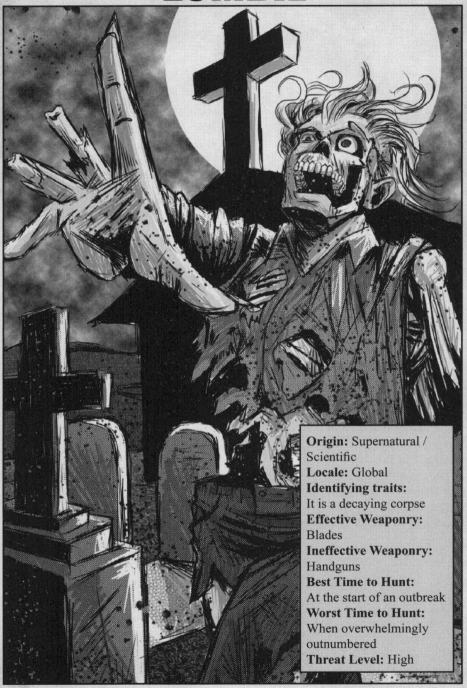

Origin: Supernatural / Scientific
Locale: Global
Identifying traits:
It is a decaying corpse
Effective Weaponry:
Blades
Ineffective Weaponry:
Handguns
Best Time to Hunt:
At the start of an outbreak
Worst Time to Hunt:
When overwhelmingly outnumbered
Threat Level: High

A mindless, soulless, reanimated corpse that carries an infection that will create others of its kind through a transference into human blood in the form of a bite.

Zombies have evolved.
The Monster Hunter's combat techniques must evolve as well.

Stories of Zombie-like creatures rising from the dead date back to 1,000 years B.C. in the Epic of Gilgamesh, but most of what we know of these poor wretches comes from more recent encounters. For our purposes, there are two classifications of Zombie: The Mystical Zombie and the Modern Zombie. Mystical Zombies arose from the Vodoo practices of Africa and Haiti where Bogors would call upon a reanimated corpse as a slave to do their bidding. These Zombies were the easiest to fight. Since it required a strong dose of dark magic to conjure up the dead, most Bogors could only control one at a time. Counter spells could easily be used to render the Undead ineffectual. In a pinch, feeding the Zombie salt was another way to return it to its grave.

Modern Zombies are a Monster Hunter's main concern in this classification of Undead enemy. They are a new brand of evil grown out of some unknown laboratory in what was either a misguided attempt to study the mystical properties of the Zombie or the intentional development of a biological weapon. The birth of the modern Zombies is directly linked to the genetic engineering of a strain of virus that escaped the walls of the laboratory of its creation. These Zombies have become the far greater danger to the human species and one of the highest-risk Monsters a Hunter can encounter.

The modern Zombie is a reanimated corpse like its mystical predecessor, but these abominations do not serve a master or have any purpose at all. Their singular mission is to consume human flesh, with a particular attraction to the brain. Their bodies are in a continuous state of decay, making their individual reigns of terror relatively short-lived. The average Zombie has a maximum projected "life expectancy" of a half-dozen years.[10] But the individual Zombie is rarely the problem. Their danger comes from pure number.

10   No Zombie has ever lasted this long with trained Monster Hunters on the case. The estimate is based off the average rate of human decay.

Zombies can be identified by sight, sound, and smell ... But you should avoid taste or feel.

The modern Zombie is the result of a biological contagion, a virus that kills indiscriminately. But the real tragedy of this infection is that it does not leave its victims to rest in peace. Immediately upon death, the body revives, animated in a singular purpose: to consume human flesh. The victim no longer exists in thought or personality. The Zombie corpse is only an empty husk, with no resemblance to its former self.

The Zombie's greatest—and only—weapon is the infection that it spreads. Carried through the saliva, it transfers to the living when mixed with human blood. All it takes is one small nick of the skin for a human to become infected. The virus is a deadly toxin, killing the victim and turning him into the living dead.

The speed at which this transformation occurs depends on the severity and location of the bite, but once the poison enters the bloodstream there is no stopping it. Of course, "bite" is a relative term. Any open wound can carry the virus once infected. I, personally, have seen an inconsequential scratch on a victim's wrist become infected by a minimal amount of Zombie saliva. It was a truly fascinating sight to witness in spite of the fact that is cost me one of my more capable apprentices.

The virus attacks the motor cortex of the brain sending out impulses that keep the body in motion while the organs and other internal systems shut down causing death. At that point, the corpse is taken over by these involuntary impulses solely motivated by the need to consume flesh. There are no thoughts. No beating heart. Zombies do not feel pain or experience any awareness of danger. They will walk right into a burning building if they sense a human inside.

There is no clear reason why Zombies seek out human flesh as, being dead, they do not require energy to fuel their bodies. In fact, research has shown that overeating with no natural means of expelling the waste has a negative affect on the Zombie anatomy. Scientists have offered many different explanations for this uncontrollable urge, but since no one has come up with a definitive reason I say we leave the theorizing to science and deal with what the Monster Hunter needs to know to fight these creatures.

It is easy to identify a Zombie because it literally looks like the walking dead. There is no blending in with the population at large. The body is totally devoid of blood, leaving it even paler than the average Vampire. Being that there is no noticeable intelligence, Zombies wear a vacant expression reflecting that lack of thought. As Zombies are in a constant state of decay, there is most definitely the scent of death about them that intensifies as they decompose.

One other consequence of the decomposition process is the distinctive Zombie moan that comes from the gasses released as the body decays. The moan is an effective device for attracting other Undead to their location, but it is not a natural means of communication. Zombies can hear the moan and react to the sound of their brethren, but they do not intentionally use it to call others.

Zombies do not carry weapons or have any particularly superhuman strength or abilities. The danger of Zombies comes from the fact that they singularly focused on consuming human flesh and are often overwhelming in number during an outbreak. When they are injured, their wounds do not heal, but they also are not a deterrent. It is not unusual to see a Zombie shuffling along missing entire limbs. It is only when the spinal cord is severed during decapitation that the electrical pulses no longer flow, rendering the Zombie inert.

Zombies stop at nothing short of a severed head.

Containment is the most important element of any Zombie fight. When the Monster Hunter arrives in the area of infestation, the first thing to do is evacuate all living humans—if that has not already occurred as a natural result of the panic. The evacuation process must be carefully undertaken to keep any Zombies from escaping with the living to continue spreading the virus.

Be prepared to face the challenge of forcing the living to leave behind their relatives and friends that have turned. Many misguided humans believe that some spark of their loved one might remain in the Zombie corpse. It is best to be compassionate in this case, but at a certain point force may become necessary in removing the living. You do not need them turning and adding to the problem. It's also good to choose a secondary site to contain and observe the evacuees in case any of them have been infected so the virus does not continue to spread uncontrolled.

Once the living are cleared, it is imperative that the area is locked down so that the Zombies cannot escape. Rogue Zombies can quickly turn a local problem into a worldwide epidemic. For this reason I highly recommend that Zombie combat be a team activity.

Zombies are naturally attracted to human flesh, so it is unlikely that you will need to hunt them in the traditional sense. They will come to you. Conveniently, as they do not possess intelligence and have no ability to recognize danger, one-on-one Zombie combat is quite direct. The goal is to remove the head from the body, severing the spine. That is the only way to stop of Zombie.[11]

---

11   Unlike Vampires, there is no need to bury the head separately
          from the body. Once the spine is severed, the threat ceases to exist.

Basic hand weapons are the most useful tools in Zombie combat. Anything with a sharp enough edge will be sufficient in the task of severing the head, so long as there is enough strength behind it. Your best bet is power tools, like a chainsaw, to compensate for any hesitancy the person wielding it may experience. A secondary method for fighting the dead is crushing the brain with a bludgeoning tool, like a hammer or mallet. Larger guns can also slow a Zombie, but only projectiles powerful enough to completely take off a head will be of real use.

Some Monster Hunters argue that setting fire to a Zombie can destroy the corpse and sever the connections that animate the body. While it is true that flames will have that effect on the body, it is not an expedient process. One time, while fighting Zombies in a small village in Italy, one of my more headstrong pupils decided to test this theory against my direct order. The Zombie was successfully lit aflame, but continued on undaunted, spreading the fire to his Zombie brethren, the entire village, and my now late apprentice. Yes, the threat was eventually contained, but at a great cost to life and property. Cutting off the head is faster, safer, and, quite honestly, a hell of a lot more effective.

Fighting the individual Zombie is not a difficult task. So long as you stay clear of the mouth, the average Monster Hunter can take out a single Zombie with little muss or fuss. The problem is that there is rarely such a thing as a single Zombie.

By the time a Monster Hunter arrives at an outbreak, the virus has usually spread. Even when fighting in teams, it is easy to become overwhelmed by this enemy. In that case it is imperative that you remember the most important rule in Zombie combat: When outnumbered, find an escape route and retreat. As Zombies move at a slower speed than humans, all you need to do is outpace them so that you can regroup and resume the attack.

Note: A recent mutation in the virus has led to a strain that creates what have become known as "Super Zombies" that are stronger and faster than the average slow-walking Zombie. The properly trained Monster Hunter will still maintain an advantage on these Zombies, but they are a larger threat to the more sedentary population at large. I have been tracking this mutation of the virus. If it ever reaches a global level then the much dreaded Zombie Apocalypse will be upon us, damning us all. For this reason, Zombies have outpaced Vampires as the Monster Hunters' greatest threat.

Ghoul

Few creatures a Monster Hunter will encounter have inspired more debate about their true nature than the Ghoul. Even Vampires, with their numerous conflicting mythologies are not the cause of as much confusion because at the core, everyone can agree that all Vampires have the same basic traits. There is very little consensus on what, exactly, a Ghoul is. This is especially true in terms of how we should deal with one. Unsurprisingly, they are among the least encountered Monsters on the planet.

In a historical context, the idea of the Ghoul originated in Middle Eastern mythology as a demon or evil jinn that lured its victims—most often children—into the desert to kill them. The Ghouls of folklore were shapeshifters that could take the form of animals (primarily scavengers) that would eat the dead and haunt burial grounds. Though there is no modern record of these mystical Ghouls existing any longer, it is believed that the mythology was conscripted to explain this new breed of creature that dwells in cemeteries where it consumes the rotting flesh of the dead.

Contrary to popular belief, Ghouls today are not synonymous with Zombies. Though there are many similarities between these animated corpses, it is their differences that are most important to note. Zombies feast on living flesh, while Ghouls are solely focused on feeding off the dead. They are no threat to the living, but the horrific manner in which they defile the bodies and memories of loved ones who have passed have generated no small amount of understandable hatred for them.

Ghouls also cannot reanimate the dead or turn living humans into the Undead like Zombies, which is another trait that has lead to confusion over the origin of these creatures. It is possible that they are another, even rarer, mutation of the Zombie virus, which is why we have included them in this section, but that is only conjecture.

What we do know is that Ghouls present very little challenge in combat. They can be destroyed through a simple decapitation, but the question remains whether or not they should be fought at all.

Personally, I feel that Ghouls should be captured, not murdered. Their horror comes from the desecration of the dead. The only danger they present is the potential for panic since civilians tend to overreact to mysterious beings in the cemetery dining on grandma's remains. In that respect, Ghouls need to be captured as much for their own sake as for the population at large. Keeping Ghouls in containment where they are fed a diet of carrion will render them completely harmless.

The Undead are a fascinating cross-section of natural, supernatural, and scientific creations. As we have learned, they each have different strengths, weaknesses, and motivations. It is my hope that you now have a better understand of what makes them tick and how to keep them from ticking. But this information is just the beginning of your education into Monster Hunting. Where you take your training from here is up to you.

Where I will take it from here is onto the fascinating subject of crypto zoology and the fabulous beasties that inhabit our planet. These living creatures that defy rational explanation will test our most basic understanding of the Hunt. I'm not talking about stalking deer or ducks. This prey is far more exciting and far more deadly. Next, we move onto the Cryptids…

CRYPTIDS

The Boy Scouts got it right: Be Prepared.

Monster Hunters are exposed to some of the most fantastical and terrifying creatures ever imagined. Generations have shared their tales, blending fact with fiction until reality became little more than nightmare. As we've already discussed, the goal of this Survival Guide is to prepare you for your encounters with the unknown. To arm you with the knowledge to defend yourself and others while facing these supposedly mythological creatures. In our previous examination of the Undead, we spent most of our time dealing with the Monsters of supernatural or scientific origin. Even in the natural case, we dealt with some very unnatural situations. Now we move on to the Monsters of the natural world.

Cryptozoology is the study of the fabulous beasties that pepper our histories as tall tales and folklore. Specifically, it is the scientific study of these "hidden" animals that science has yet to prove actually exist. The media would have us believe that this is the science of crackpots. That these people are wasting their time trying to prove the impossible. Debunking these stories is a long-standing tradition for the legitimate news media, but not for the reasons you might think. The media has long known about the existence of many of these creatures, but there has always been an understanding between them and the government that spreading the news of these Monsters could cause panic among the populace. As a result, a carefully constructed fiction has been created by major news organizations to only reveal what is in the public's best interest.

Cryptids, as they are called, put the "hunt" in Monster Hunter. They are the beasts that burden us and their capture (or kill) is more like a traditional hunt than your dealings with the Undead. But these are not mere rabbits, ducks, or deer that good ol' boys track down on weekends with oversized weapons as a display of their manhood. These vicious Monsters hunt back. Unlike lions or tigers, these predators can't always be taken out by a big gun. The worst of them will do more than just take a bite out of you. Some of them like to play with their food first.

To prepare for the hunt you must be well armed. This is true of any Monster you will track. But you will carry more than just guns and knives. The properly prepared Monster Hunter always has a varied selection of items within arm's reach to deal with anything that comes at him.

Never leave home with the basic essentials.

Whether stalking a Sasquatch or recording a ghostly haunting there are certain basic items that every Monster Hunter should carry at all times. The most successful Hunters are always prepared to leave for a Hunt on a moment's notice. I suggest always having two emergency packs stored inside the front door to your home. The first pack is for equipment and clothing: All items that you can carry on the plane without incident. The second pack is for weapons. Airlines have strict policies about transporting weaponry. Familiarize yourself with those rules before travel to avoid any unnecessary delays. There is nothing worse than arriving at your destination to take on a Werewolf only to find that all your silver bullets have been confiscated.

The equipment pack should contain the following:

Up-To-Date Passport

Cell Phone And Emergency Contact
Not just a next of kin, you should always have a backup on speed dial ready to come save your ass.

Notepad And Pencil Or Pen

Watch With A Second Hand
Preferably an old fashioned wind-up version. Electromagnetic activity associated with certain supernatural beings can affect batteries.

Flashlight
Wind-up survival flashlights are the new fad, but don't forget to bring extra batteries

Binoculars

Compass

GPS

First Aid Kit
Basic medical supplies, including anti-venom, are a must. My kit also contains a cyanide pill for extreme situations.

Candles and matches

Chalk

Basic Spell Book

Walk softly and carry a big stick ... along with a fully stocked arsenal.

In an ideal situation, it's best to arm yourself with weapons specific to the Monster you will encounter, since a wooden stake is pretty useless against the Kraken. But any Monster Hunter will tell you there is no such thing as an ideal situation. Failing that, the best-prepared Hunters are armed to the teeth and stash a cache of weapons for backup in the field of battle.

A Monster Hunter should have the following weapons on his or her body at all times:

Semi-Automatic Pistol and extra magazines
Loaded with traditional ammunition, but also carry a clip with silver bullets.

Hunting Knife

Silver dagger

Silver Sword
Carried in a hilt strapped to the back for ease of movement. (Optional)

Shurikens (Throwing Stars)

Wooden stake[1]

Hand Grenade

It's always good to travel light, but you have to balance the need for maneuverability with safety. The following weapons do not have to be on your body at all times, but it is highly recommended that they be in reach.

Shotgun
With traditional ammunition and silver bullets.

Machine gun
With traditional and silver bullets.

Crossbow

Throwing Axe

High and Low Explosives

Salt

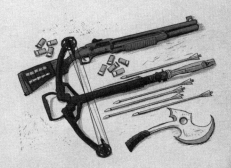

---

1.   Vampires are often drawn to trouble and can surprise you at the worst moment. Besides, a stake to the heart of a Yeti is just as lethal as it is to a Vampire.

Bigfoot/Sasquatch

Origin: Natural
Locale: Forests & Mountains of U.S. Pacific Northwest and Canadian West
Identifying traits: Shaggy reddish-brown hair covering entire body
Effective Weaponry: Shotgun
Ineffective Weaponry: Knives
Best Time to Hunt: Evening and Morning
Worst Time to Hunt: Night
Threat Level: Moderate

A large, bipedal, hairy hominoid. Predominantly found in the Pacific Northwest of the United States and Western Canada.

The name may change, but the threat remains the same.

Some Monsters go by many names, given to them by the different civilizations across the globe that have encountered their species. They have their own histories. Their own mythologies. Their own truths. This is the way it is with many Monsters, but none more so than the one we know best as Bigfoot.

Admittedly, the name "Bigfoot" does not strike fear in the hearts of the average human. It doesn't have the ancient feel to it as a Ferla Mohr of Scotland or Chuchunya of Siberia. The tribal elegance of the Apamandi of Zaire or Baramanu of Pakistan. Or even the stately grace of The Gray King of Wales. But there is no question that Bigfoot is the most familiar of these bipedal hominoids that walk the forests nightly in search of prey.

The Canadians call it a Sasquatch, which was adapted from the name the indigenous tribes gave them: sokqueatl and soss-q'tal. Many in the scientific community prefer this moniker for the creature as it sounds more "scientific." As far as I'm concerned, it doesn't matter what you call it so long as you know how to deal with it. Personally, I like Bigfoot. The name perfectly captures its most distinguishing feature, which is useful in tracking the beast.

The story of these Wildmen exists in numerous Native American tribes dating back centuries, although the name "Bigfoot" is a more recent development. Sightings of the Cryptid were prevalent during the twentieth century and the name "Big Foot" had been used colloquially to describe the tracks of the creature. In the late 1950s a set of large tracks cited to be from the local "apeman" were found over the course of several days on a construction site in Northern California. As proof of the phenomenon, the witness and a friend made a plaster cast of the print, showing the "Big Foot"—as the locals had been calling it—off to the press. When the small town, local media printed the story, the reporter condensed the word to "Bigfoot" and it has forever since been known by that name.

Sometimes the simple truths are most telling.
For example: Bigfoot has big feet.

In addition to their oversized feet Bigfoot creatures are almost as famous for their skills of concealment. This has led to much debate about their existence over the decades, allowing the government to debunk the stories so that we can do our jobs without curious onlookers getting in the way.

Anyone setting out to track Bigfoot should begin with its most recognizable trait. The creature's feet are elongated, running fourteen to sixteen inches in length and an average eight inches wide. Prints reveal a double-muscled ball and a pronounced heel. The stride is twice that of the average human. Some reports claim that they only have four toes, but that is incorrect. Like humans, they have five toes without claws, which is one of the many factors that distinguish their prints from bear tracks.

Bigfoot creatures are also sometimes mistaken for apes, which is ridiculous considering the general lack of these larger primates in the forests of North America. Their posture is considerably more human-like as that they stand almost completely erect, with only a minimal slouch. Their arms do hang lower down their sides than humans and their heads are conical, rising to a rounded point.

Bigfoot creatures run seven to nine feet tall and can weigh as much as five hundred pounds at the extreme. Shaggy hair covers their entire body, except for their faces, the palms of their hands and the soles of their feet. The color of this hair changes as they age, beginning as a darker brown and then fading into a reddish-brown as they reach maturity. Older Bigfoot creatures have been reported as having silver hair, though I have never encountered any. When you know what you're looking for, it is easy to follow the tufts of hair left behind on trees or bushes they have brushed up against. This hair is distinctly different from the fur of the typical forest animals.

Relying on all your senses to track the Monster, another notable trait is the strong odor, often described as being similar to burnt hair. They also emit high-pitched whistles and howls, but no clear language has been recognized.

Bigfoot creatures are well practiced at using their surroundings as camouflage, often hiding in plain sight simply by standing against a tree. This is usually good enough to fool the average hiker, but any Monster Hunter that can be taken in by such a basic concealment technique seriously needs to reconsider this line of work.

*Sticks and stones may break your bones,
so it's usually best to avoid them.*

Bigfoot creatures are shy animals that primarily feast on plant life and fish. They are solitary beings, preferring to live alone, although there have been unconfirmed reports of families of Bigfoot sighted. In spite of those rumors, all evidence points to the fact that what they mainly desire in life is to be left alone. Regretfully, with the unchecked growth of cities and towns across the country, the natural habitat of Bigfoot creatures has come under threat in recent decades. As a result, a few of these otherwise docile creatures have reportedly lashed out against interlopers perceived as threatening their home. In spite of these scattered reports of growing aggression in the Bigfoot community, there have been very few recorded instances of a Bigfoot killing a human. .

To stem the aggressive behavior in these creatures, I have been working with the U.S. Government to establish the first official protected Bigfoot habitat in North America. The clandestine location has been chosen with these animals in mind, taking into account their dietary needs as well as their preference for solitude. To that end, all Monster Hunters should work to relocate these creatures instead of Hunting them out of existence.

Bigfoot creatures are primarily nocturnal, which is another key factor of their clandestine existence. When working to capture and relocate a Bigfoot creature, I suggest you avoid tracking them in the darkest parts of the night. You are working on their home turf when you enter the forest and should not put yourself at a disadvantage. Stick to the earlier evening and morning. Always have a pair of night vision goggles to compensate for the fact that even the full moon cannot penetrate the densest parts of the forest.

Food and water are the most easily exploited weakness as their diet consists heavily on fish. Bigfoot creatures can often be found near rivers and lakes, so it is recommended that these spots are the best locations for laying a trap.

Another important facet to consider when tracking a Bigfoot creature is that they possess intelligence. It is a limited intelligence, but definitely more than your basic dumb animal. Bigfoot creatures can use rudimentary weaponry and often hurl rocks and stones when they feel threatened. If you are unable to take the Bigfoot by surprise, it is best to keep your distance. What they lack in aim, they make up for in pure strength in the ability to fling heavy boulders quite far.

Bigfoot is deceptively strong and can easily subdue even the strongest Hunter. It is not wise to approach them as they perceive that as an act of aggression. Stronger tranquilizer guns are recommended with steel darts to get the sedative into the bloodstream. Their hair is not particularly thick, but their hides are tough. Transporting these creatures is also a two-person operation as they are quite cumbersome and remember to monitor their vital signs to ensure that you do not needlessly cause them harm.

Yeti

Among the many "cousins" to the North American Bigfoot, none are better known than the Yeti found in the Himalayan Mountains of Nepal and Tibet. The name is derived from the word Yeh-Teh, which roughly translates to "that thing." A mistranslation of the language has lead to the more common nickname for the beast: The Abominable Snowman.

No one can agree on the number of different species of Yeti, but that does not matter for our purposes. They all share common traits that make them indistinguishable for hunting. As they almost all live above the snowline of the Himalayas, it is difficult to get an accurate account on the shape of their footprints as snow can be unreliable at recording the imprint. Some people have confused the oversized footprints with snowshoes, however sometimes distinct toes can be made out.[2]

The most common misconception about the Yeti is the idea that their hair is white. They are, in fact, similar to Bigfoot in this respect as well. Yetis have dark brown hair covering their bodies, which lightens to reddish-brown with aging. The one distinguishing fact is that some have white patches of hair on their chests, but this is rather unimportant in the grand scheme of things. You see a big, hairy hominoid on the mountaintop, the odds are it's a Yeti.

2.   With the temperatures often below freezing, it is unlikely to find many humans going barefoot on the mountains.

Yetis are as strong and powerful as Bigfoot, with the larger members of the species able to take down a yak. However, unlike Bigfoot, the Yeti are dangerously aggressive creatures. Legend attributes their bloodthirsty behavior with their nearly being hunted to extinction during the time of Genghis Khan. In fact, among certain historians, the Yetis are believed to be one of the contributing factors in Khan's inability to extend his empire south of the Himalayas. This has resulted in the creatures becoming truly threatening to anyone that enters their habitat.

Their diet is more heavily carnivorous, preferring human or animal meat to fish, which is not plentiful at the higher elevations. Though they are bipedal, some move as quadrupeds, often reaching speeds similar to a Mustang. They often move in pairs, so take special care when approaching one as its mate is surely in the area and they will work together to defend themselves.

When combating a Yeti, remember that the air is thinner at higher elevations and it is easier to run out of oxygen with only minimal exertion. Humans must also take special care to insulate themselves against the cold, while Yetis are perfectly comfortable in their natural climate. One benefit that you do have with this environment is that the dark brown hair of the Yeti does stand out against the snow.

Climbing experience is a must and the ability to use traditional equipment for scaling a mountain while carrying weaponry is an absolute necessity. This means you'll have to travel light, with minimal firepower. I'd also suggest hiring a Sherpa as a guide. Though the locals have an understandable fear of these Monsters, I've found that the proper amount of money can soothe even the most jangled nerves.

Mongolian Death Worm

The Mongolian Death Worm is an invertebrate burrowing animal with a large, slender body found in the Gobi Desert of Mongolia and China. Known regionally as Allghoi khorkhoi, or "intestine worm" for its resemblance to cow intestines, its body can grow longer than five feet and be thicker than a human arm. The creature is blood red in color with black spots and spiky, horn-like growths at both ends of its body that circle the tips almost like teeth.

The Mongolian Death Worm is a deceptively powerful being, considering it appears to be little more than an overgrown worm. As the land of the Gobi desert is mostly a rocky plateau and not sand, those feelers are strong enough to navigate the underground and send the Worm bursting out of the earth toward unsuspecting victims.

It can kill from a distance by spitting an acidic poison on its victims. The yellow poison instantly corrodes anything it touches. Reportedly, the spray can emit from either end of the body and has a reach of about six to eight feet, so remember to keep at least that much distance between yourself and the creature in your encounters. I suggest firearms, arrows, or throwing stars or axes as the weapons of choice. Touching the Worm's skin can also bring a painful death from the acid that emits from its pores, so you should never engage it in physical combat.

The Monster also emits an electric shock that has been known to kill, but more often than not merely incapacitates the victim long enough for the poison to do its work. This too seems to have an effective distance of up to eight feet. Once the victim is dead or disabled, the worm will set to work devouring the meal at a leisurely pace. In this respect, the worm is snake-like. Once it has you in its clutches it is almost impossible to break free. If a victim is not dead by the time he is being devoured, I strongly suggest putting the poor soul out of his misery.

Due to the extreme cold temperatures of the Gobi Desert, the worm lies dormant in the winter, living exclusively beneath the surface. Most encounters occur during the warmest months of June and July. They often come out after a rain or when the ground is wet, making that the prime hunting time.

Tracking the Mongolian Death Worm can be difficult due to the fact that it moves exclusively underground. Wormholes, however, are notable for their size and shape as well as the acidic residue left behind when the creature enters and exits the ground. Again, take care while examining the holes as the acid remains lethal for hours. It is believed that the color yellow attracts the worm, but I have yet to see this in practice.

Unlike some mysterious beings that skeptics question the validity of, sightings of the Mongolian Death Worm are plentiful. More often, the burrow holes it leaves behind remain as clear evidence of its existence. This creature has terrified the region for centuries. Tribesmen consider the mere mention of its name as bad luck so take care when interviewing the locals as you do not want to alienate your most useful resources on the hunt.

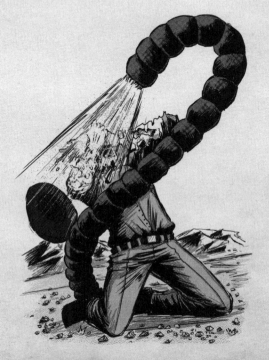

Thunderbird

Like so many of the creatures we encounter, the key element in combating the Thunderbird is the ability to separate fact from fiction. The Thunderbird is a major figure in the mythology of almost all North American indigenous peoples. Though the stories of this Avian Monster varied dramatically between the different Native American tribes, the Thunderbird was uniformly believed to be sent to protect the people from evil.

The Thunderbird has been described as condor-like, alternately having the body of a winged-human or that of a giant bird. In some cases, it was believed to be a shape-shifter that could become human. There are several tales of it falling in love and marrying in this guise. The supernatural being was believed to be the personification of thunder where the beating of its wings would stir the winds and cause the air to rumble. It created lightning with the blink of its eyes and could generate disturbances above and below the earth.

If any of this were true, I'd advise you to steer as clear of the Thunderbird as possible. Luckily for us, these tall tales are greatly exaggerated versions of a Cryptid that is relatively easy to combat. Traditional hunting techniques are all that are needed, so long as you're packing the proper amount of firepower.

The Thunderbird of our reality is most likely a cousin to the condor. A very large cousin, but an earthly being nonetheless. Some reports claim that it is featherless and lizard-like, however most experts believe this is due to confusion with the African Kongamato[3]. Thunderbirds can be found in the forests and plains of North America with the highest concentration located in the Appalachian Mountains. The best time for hunting is during their migration in late March and early August.

Thunderbirds are roughly eight feet tall when perched, but unfold to a twenty-foot wingspan while in flight. Their grasping talons are sharper and stronger than most winged animals and must be avoided at all costs. They are vicious predators known for their lifting ability that eclipses most birds, allowing them to carry off livestock and small children, returning them to their nesting area as meals.

Heavier firearms are suggested when dealing with these large birds. A simple arrow or pistol will not take them down. At minimum a double-barreled shotgun is recommended, though you'll only get one shot before scaring the Thunderbird off, so make sure your aim is good.

They are not particularly fast creatures, but their enormous wings can carry them up to higher altitudes, rendering even the most powerful projectiles inadequate in spite of the large target that they present. They do make their nesting grounds in mountaintop caves and I've found sneaking up on them while grounded is a better option. Weighted netting made of airline cable is useful to trap the giant birds so they cannot fly off. While I admit that it's not as sporting to kill a trapped animal, you must remember that, fun as Monster Hunting can be, you're not in it as a hobby. Protecting the Thunderbird's victims should be your sole concern.

3.   Which we will discuss shortly

Kongamato

The Kongamato is believed to be a descendant of Pterosaurs, flying reptiles from prehistoric times. Though they have been reported in various locales, the highest known concentrations of these flying lizards are in Africa, particularly in the areas of Mount Kilimanjaro and Mount Kenya. They have been called flying dragons in spite of the fact that they have no direct relationship to the far more dangerous species.

These nocturnal creatures are most often described as a lizard with the wings of a bat and a long tail. Their leathery, featherless wings can reach a span of up to eight feet and their heads boast long beaks full of sharp teeth that can rip into animal flesh easily. They are either red or black in coloring and are most likely to be seen at dusk or dawn though they are quite active at night.

Kongamato are attracted to swampy areas, though that is not their exclusive hunting ground. Their primary diet is fish, but they do have a taste for flesh and have been seen digging up shallow graves with their claws to feed on the dead. Unlike Ghouls, however, they have rarely been mistaken for demons in spite of their attraction to rotting flesh. They do avoid live human prey, although they do not fear man and will not shy away from attack. They are especially dangerous toward fishermen perceived to be invading their hunting ground.

The name Kongamato means "overwhelmer of boats," as that is their preferred method of dealing with humans they deem to be encroaching on their territory. More than a few fishermen have drowned under their relentless attack. The indigenous people carry charms to protect themselves while crossing waterways, but this is nothing more than local superstition and has no basis in fact.

Kongamato present very little challenge to the average Monster Hunter and are seen by many as more akin to hunting for sport. Since these creatures are rarely dangerous to humans unless their territory is threatened, I prefer capturing the animals and relocating them to uninhabited areas in place of killing them. For this task, a non-lethal net launcher is recommended, preferably firing a net constructed from nylon covered aircraft cable as the sharp claws of the Kongamato have been known to shred traditional rope. Once the creature is netted, a mild tranquilizer will be suitable to prepare it for travel.

Ahool

Often confused with the flying-lizard, Kongamato, the Ahool is far more bat-like in its appearance and likely a member of the order Chiroptera. With a body the size of a human infant, the Ahool has dark gray fur and a head similar to a macaque or gibbon. For this reason, some believe it to be a flying primate. The creature has large, dark wings that can stretch from six to ten feet, which is almost twice as long as its nearest relative in the family of bats. Another notable feature are the large, grasping claws at the tops of its forearms that make up part of its wings. These claws are not particularly strong or dangerous to humans, but they are useful at snatching fish out of a river.

The Ahool takes its name from the "hooool" sound that it makes, which is also the reason it is sometimes mistaken for a giant owl when not confused with the Kongamato. Needless to say, there is very little recorded evidence of the creature, though I have seen it with my own eyes and can confirm its existence. The nocturnal animal is indigenous to the rainforests of Western Java and can often be found near rivers, where its primary source of food is fish.[4]

Sightings of the Ahool have caused panic in the witnesses due mainly to the pure size of the Cryptid. Humans are, by nature, afraid of the unknown and a giant bat-like animal is exactly the type of thing that we have been trained to fear since childhood. Aside from their frightful appearance, I believe that part of this fear comes from the fictional stories that link bats to Vampires. Certainly, the Ahool has not been helped by the negative press that is an offshoot of fertile minds.

Let me make it clear that there are no recorded instances of an Ahool attacking humans or causing them direct harm in any way. That's not to say that they are entirely docile creatures. They will become aggressive during breeding season and try to scare off intruders with threatening behavior. This is limited to swooping down on people and buzzing them. Rarely do they ever make contact, and even when they do, their claws are not strong or sharp enough to do any real damage. In my opinion, it is better to just leave this creature alone as there are far more dangerous predators to deal with.

4.   This makes the Ahool different from the majority of bats that mostly feed off insects and fruit.

Loch Ness Monster

Origin: Natural
Locale: Loch Ness, Scotland
Identifying traits: Serpent-like head rising from water
Effective Weaponry: Cameras
Ineffective Weaponry: Anything that would cause the Monster harm
Threat Level: Low

Known by the familiar name, "Nessie," this Lake Monster is a member of the Plesiosaur family of marine reptiles and one of the most popular Cryptids of modern times.

Don't believe the hype.

The Loch Ness Monster, or "Nessie" as she has become known, is one of the most famous Cryptids in the world. She is believed to be a member of the Plesiosaur family of marine reptiles that became extinct during the Cretaceous–Tertiary extinction event.[5] While most likely a descendant of the Plesiosaur, some researchers have theorized that it is possible she is an actual survivor of the event and could predate man by millions of years. This would make her one of the longest-lived creatures on the planet.

There have been a number of reported sightings of the Loch Ness Monster over the years, but the industry of hoaxes that has grown around Nessie are almost as abundant as the actual witness reports. When you examine these sightings, certain traits become common, giving us the true picture of the mysterious Cryptid that I, personally, have confirmed the existence of through several encounters. In fact, I suspect that I have unintentionally become the foremost expert on the subject, having interacted with the Loch Ness Monster on more occasions than any other human.

Nessie's gray body stretches for thirty feet from the tip of her horse-like head to the end of her tail. Though there are reports that she has anywhere from one to three humps on her back, I can confirm that there are exactly two, rising only slightly higher than her back and only really becoming noticeable when the humps are the only part of her body rising out of the water. Her serpentine neck is generally the cause of most sightings as she raises her head above the waterline while her flippers propel her across Loch Ness.

Some believe Nessie to be a Kelpie.[6] The mythological Kelpie is a shape-shifting water spirit that can take many forms, but is most often associated with the body of a hairy man or a horse grazing by the edge of the river. It uses these disguises to attract unwary travelers, taking on an attractive male form to entice women while in horse form it lures humans to ride it. As a horse, it traps its rider and pulls him down into the water. Depending on the story, the purpose of this deception can be to merely dunk the victim, drown him, or devour him. These tales could not be further from the truth of the Loch Ness Monster, which has proven to be one of the few truly docile Monsters in the world.

I debated strongly whether to even include Nessie in this tome, but I do it as a reminder to all Monster Hunters that just because something is different does not mean that it is our enemy.

---

5. However, these creatures were likely cold-blooded and could not survive in the waters of Loch Ness, which have an average temperature of forty-two degrees Fahrenheit.
6. Also known as a Water Horse.

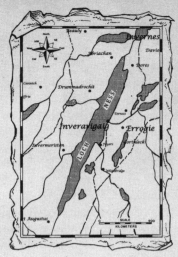

Ancient is not the same as Old.

Loch Ness, located in the Scottish Highlands, is a freshwater lake approximately twenty-four miles long and only about a mile and a half wide at its largest points. With a large population of salmon and trout, it is a bountiful feeding ground for Nessie. Its average depth is approximately 400 feet with it dropping down to 900 feet at some points. These measurements make it the third largest body of freshwater in Europe by volume. The depth of the lake along with the inky quality to the water that makes it nearly impossible to see more than a few feet beneath the surface are the prime factors explaining how a Lake Monster, like Nessie, could remain a mystery for such a long time.

It has been estimated that Loch Ness was formed following the last ice age, ten thousand years ago, having been frozen for the prior twenty thousand years. This has led some to propose that the Loch Ness Monster may have been on ice during that time and trapped in the lake when the ice melted and the waters receded. The current denizen of the deep may be a descendant of that Cryptid or the very creature itself.

The Monster's longevity is substantiated by stone carvings dating back to the first century A.D. made by the indigenous tribe known as the Picts. The first recorded mention of the Loch Ness Monster can be found in a sixth century tale of The Life of St. Columba. According to the story, St. Columba, a missionary monk who introduced Christianity to the Picts, converted a man-eating serpent into a shy Monster in the waters of Loch Ness. Whether or not the Monster was docile before its alleged encounter with the monk is not as important as the fact that history has confirmed the nature of the creature for centuries.

The stories of Nessie may date back all these many centuries, but the bulk of the reported sightings have occurred within the past hundred years. This is likely due to road construction around the loch in the 1930s that increased traffic in the area, bringing more people to the lake. The stories of the Loch Ness Monster coming out of the area increased awareness of Nessie, making the lake a prime destination for those seeking to explain the unexplained, turning it into a popular tourist destination. Over the years, there have been several pieces of photographic evidence of the creature, though skeptics believe these to be fakes.

Clearly Nessie is not an air-breather or, even with the size of the lake, there would be more sightings considering the pure number of spectators on the hunt. Sonar studies of the lake have revealed submerged animals roughly twenty feet in length, but have been inconclusive in scientifically proving the existence of the Monster.

What the public knows of Nessie beyond the agreed upon physical description is what is seen the few times she peeks her head above the surface. A distinctive V-wave cuts through the water announcing the rise of the Monster, though it is rare that more than the head will surface. Some reports claim that Nessie has been sighted on land, but I believe these to be false as she has never come out of the waters in my experiences with her, which brings me to the subject of my interactions with Nessie.

I can confirm that the Monster is shy, like the story of St. Columba tells us. It took me several visits to earn her trust enough to bring her to the water's edge to interact with me. I did this to confirm the rumors of her placid nature to cross her off the list on Monsters we should concern ourselves with. I would prefer not to reveal my methods for attracting her here, for fear of someone with impure intentions using them for their own benefit. Suffice to say, it was a challenge that I deftly managed. I've journeyed back to Loch Ness numerous times since our first meeting and found Nessie to be completely docile and, actually, a pleasurable companion. She has a distinctly playful personality once out of her metaphorical shell and can be a welcome distraction from the often solitary life of the Monster Hunter.

Bunyip

In spite of its non-threatening name and the fact that the mythology surrounding the Monster has inspired popular children's book characters, the Bunyip is one of the most dangerous Cryptids a Monster Hunter can encounter. It is an amphibious creature indigenous to Australia believed to be a descendant of the marsupial Diprotodon, or giant wombat, which was the largest marsupial known to man.

The Bunyip was first mentioned in various Aboriginal mythologies, though the stories varied dramatically on the look of the Monster. Some have suggested that the creature was a shape-shifter to account for the various descriptions ranging from it being a huge, hairy snake to it having a human body with a bird's head and possibly a duck bill. Other sightings have claimed that it has the tail of a crocodile while the rest of its body resembles that of an emu or bandicoot with its feet turned backwards.

I've encountered enough Bunyips in my career that I can proudly claim for the first time in print that most prevalent reports are accurate. The Bunyip is a large-bodied marsupial covered in dark, shaggy fur, with a head that has canine features and tusks, long arms that end in sharp claws, and a tail similar to a horse's. They can grow to seven feet long and weigh up to an impressive eight hundred pounds.

Bunyips are fiercely territorial, inhabiting swamps, creeks, billabongs, and similar areas where water collects. Their prey consists of any animal or human that has ventured too close to their home. They attack without warning, dragging their prey into the depths where the lucky ones drown before they are consumed. Bunyip cries can be heard at night as they attack, driving people away from dangerous waters.

Attempting to encounter the Bunyip in its home is a fool's mission. Bunyips are experts at using the familiar surroundings to their benefit, which I learned after the unfortunate loss of several apprentices over the years. The only safe way to combat the Bunyip is to lure it away from its home, onto dry land. It is still a threat due to its size, strength, and claws, but so long as you are away from the water, you are on more equal footing. The best lure I have found is the simulated cry of a wounded animal. The promise of an easy dinner lures the animal beyond what it might normally consider a safe distance from the waters.

Once the Bunyip is out in the open, I suggest a large caliber gun, or "elephant gun" for maximum firepower to pierce its thick hide. Although I do recommend at least once in your life taking on a Bunyip in physical combat armed only with a hunting knife. It is one of the most exhilarating experiences I have ever had. The loss of the little toe on my right foot was well worth it.

Who needs the Pinky Toe?

Sea Serpent

Sea Serpents are exactly what their names describe: giant snakes of the sea. They range in size from the "manageable" smaller serpents that are barely fifty feet long and fifteen inches in diameter to the more fittingly monstrous two hundred feet long and twenty feet thick. On average, they tend to be around eighty to one hundred feet from nose to tail. At least the dead ones fished out of the sea are mostly that length. It's difficult to get a good measure while they are living as their bodies are sometimes bunched up as they move through the water. Their scales are darker on the top while lighter on the underbelly and their heads are more akin to the traditional image of a dragon rather than a snake.

Sea Serpents live in caves along the shoreline and have been found in oceans all around the world, in all different temperatures of seas. Unlike traditional water snakes, Sea Serpents propel themselves by undulating vertically across the water, stretching and recoiling in an accordion-like manner. One of the more interesting facts about them is that they are the only water snake that submerges by sinking straight down into the water instead of diving.

They are known to devour anything in their path, feasting on fish, humans, and, in rare cases, the boats their food is in. Mostly, their attacks are direct, going straight in for a meal, using their sharp teeth to tear into a victim and make quick work at dispatching them. In some cases, they have taken a page from other denizens of the deep and used their muscular bodies to wrap around boats, crushing them to release their victims into the sea where they become helpless snacks.

Fighting Sea Serpents—and any Sea Monsters for that matter—requires a boat at the very least. The more timid among us prefer helicopters to keep themselves removed from the action, but this makes them relatively useless once the beast submerges. I suggest a fully armed submersible is the way to go, though these are often outside of the budget for the average Monster Hunter. In that case it is good to have a backer supporting your Hunt. Of course, when a Sea Monster is terrorizing a port town, you might be surprised by how willing the residents are to donate equipment.

Bullets have little effect on the larger Sea Serpents as only the most formidable ammunition is able to pierce the scales. Depth charges work to get the Serpent to the surface, weakening it enough for combat in the process. If you can get close to the Serpent, an explosive dropped down the throat is always good for getting to the problem from the inside.

For the smaller Serpents, sharp blades are the weapons of choice. Harpoons on a winch to start with, to pull the Serpent closer so you can slice and dice. Some ingenious Hunters have even used larger boat propellers to do the deed for them. In the end, the propellers were rendered useless, but considering the Serpent was dead, the damage to the rented boat was usually overlooked.

Kraken

Origin: Natural
Locale: Off the coasts of Norway and Iceland
Identifying traits: Huge tentacles
Effective Weaponry: Yet to be discovered
Ineffective Weaponry: Pretty much everything we've thrown at it
Best Time to Hunt: No clear answer
Worst Time to Hunt: Anytime
Threat Level: Low

A tentacled Sea Monster large enough that it can be mistaken for an island crushes ships caught in its clutches, and creates whirlpools simply by submerging.

Bigger isn't always better.

The Kraken of Scandinavian legend is the largest Sea Monster in the world. Since there have been very few survivors of a Kraken attack, it is difficult to get an exact description of the creature, but enough reports over the centuries have surfaced to give us something of an incomplete picture. What little we do know is that it has been said to be part-octopus/part-crab with anywhere from six to twelve tentacles extending from the sides of its body. For this reason it is sometimes confused with the giant squid, but this Monster is far more aggressive.

Ancient tales of the Kraken, which also goes by the names Krabben and Skykraken, report that it is a half mile in circumference with tentacles that can reach to the highest mast on the tallest of tall ships. Part of the legend also suggests that it used to lie in wait, floating atop the seas as if it were an island. Unsuspecting travelers would be deceived by its size and think that it was a perfectly safe place to land. This was the last mistake these people ever made..

The true scale of a Kraken has never been measured beyond anecdotal reports of the very few survivors. Unsurprisingly, these people were preoccupied at the time of the attack and were more concerned with survival than breaking out the measuring tape. It is believed that the Kraken is unique to the seas, being the only of its kind or, at most, one of a pair. Surely, if there were more Monsters about a half-mile in width attacking ships at sea, the sightings would be much higher than have been reported, even taking the bloodbaths that surround them into consideration.

Stories of the Kraken date back generations, so it is hard to say if this is the same creature or a descendant of the one in historical records. As the Kraken rarely emerges fully from the waters, we have no true description of the beast beyond that of its long tentacles with suckers and the gaping maw filled with multiple rows of teeth, each roughly three to five feet in length.

The Kraken is the modern Monster Hunter's White Whale.

Few Monsters have plagued the Monster Hunter more than the Kraken. To date, there is no recorded victory of a Hunter taking out this beast. Sadly, there are many instances where a Monster Hunter has given his or her life to it. As a result, the carcass of this creature has become one of the most sought after prizes of our kind.

The Kraken's main method of attack is to rise from the depths beneath a ship, and encircle the vessel with its tentacles. This was a more formidable attack in the days of wooden sailing ships, but the Kraken is incredibly strong and has been known to inflict substantial damage even to steel battleships. Smaller boats with fiberglass hulls don't stand a chance against it.

As the larger tentacles crush the ship, more slender, flexible limbs attack the personnel onboard individually, plucking them off the deck one-by-one. The victims are either dropped into the waters for retrieval later or, more likely, into its gaping maw. This is the point where the average Monster Hunter loses the battle. Since these limbs are going after the individuals onboard, it is only natural to defend yourself from the immediate attack, but this does nothing to save you from the larger threat of the Monster itself. A single Monster Hunter has no chance against the multiple arms of the beast. I believe that only a direct attack on the body of the Monster will succeed in killing it once and for all.

Once the ship is destroyed, the Kraken submerges, creating a whirlpool that will suck all remaining survivors from the surface down to the depths below where it will finish its meal. Depending on the size of the ship and number of victims, the

Kraken is often sated enough by human flesh that it can rest at the bottom of the ocean for a matter of weeks, surviving off the meal and passing sea creatures. Truthfully, it could probably live exclusively off fish and the like, but it has clearly developed a taste for human flesh, which is the only way to explain why it goes to such trouble destroying ships rather than just snacking on a passing whale.

The Kraken has shown definite signs of intelligence in the way that it hunts its prey. By vomiting smaller fish from its guts, it attracts larger fish as well as the fishermen that naturally follow. But this is nothing compared to the camouflage technique it employs to lure hapless travelers to come directly to it. Although there are no modern records of the ploy where it camouflages itself as an island, there are enough reports from the past to confirm that it was likely once employed. It's a shame really, since that would also give us a better idea of the actual body of the creature.[7]

7.   Assuming there were any survivors from the encounter, that is.

As mentioned previously, large schools of fish often precede the Kraken, which makes any bountiful fishing grounds a good place to start for tracking the Kraken. Large patches of bubbling waters in otherwise calm seas are also a good indicator. The bubbles will grow into roiling waves as it approaches the surface. While this is a good indicator that the Kraken is about to attack, it is usually too late to escape by the time this is noticed.

As no Monster Hunter has ever successfully taken down the Kraken all we can do is conjecture on the possible attack that will one day end this threat for good. Certainly explosives have been recorded doing their damage, with one report of a tentacle being blown off by a strategically placed charge. Considering that this came from a well-known braggart, I find it hard to swallow that the fool even encountered a Kraken. Surely, he would be the last person I would ever expect to survive the fight.

The Kraken has received something of pop culture resurgence in recent years. Modern films have suggested that the Kraken can be controlled or contained through human or supernatural means. This is nothing more than Hollywood story telling and should not be attempted.

I believe that the only way to successfully take on the Kraken is with a heavily armed submarine. A small, mobile submersible would be the best way to attack the goliath, going for speed and maneuverability. A steel reinforced hull will need to be electrified to shock the Kraken away should its tentacles encircle the vessel. The charge would need to be strong enough that the huge creature will feel it, without killing the crew inside. The submersible would be armed with the highest-yield explosives imaginable. I would not be averse to consider a nuclear device as the Monster presents that large of a threat. I am currently working on the design of such a vehicle and seeking backers to finance the endeavor.

It is said that the Kraken was born when the world was made and promised to exist for as long as the world exists.

We'll see about that.

Sun Tzu also got it right: Know your enemy.

The information I've provided is just a taste of what you'll need to know to take on these Monsters. Don't believe the stories and myths you may read about them online. Much of these stories were carefully planted to dissuade the casual explorers from the truth, for their protection as well as that of the creatures. While being prepared is integral to the job, nothing can compete with real world experience you will get in the field actually studying and fighting the Cryptids yourself. While I personally stand behind every fact I have printed, we are learning more about these Cryptids every day with each new sighting and the latest reports of combat. Monster Hunting works best when fighting goes hand in hand with researching, but only the research provided by the web of Monster Hunters should be trusted. Keep an ear out on official channels for any updates to this information as you move forward in your work.

The study of unusual animals does not end here, though. While I have already touched on some of the larger animals of Cryptozoological studies—including possibly the largest with the Kraken—there is an important subset that deserves a fully devoted section of their own. Next we shall explore the biggest threats in the animal world: The Giant Monsters.

GIANT MONSTERS

Know when it's time to break out the big guns.

Danger comes in all shapes and sizes. Today, most of the threats that world governments concern themselves with are microscopic. Powders, gasses, and other forms of biological warfare that can kill us and cause massive destruction are the talk of the news media. They are also responsible for creating some of the Monsters we deal with, such as Zombies. But these threats are more the concern of science, and I think you know by now how I feel about science.[1] I'm not worried about the tiniest of the tiny dangers. As Monster Hunters we focus on the big ones. The biggest ones, in fact.

People have been fascinated by Giant Monsters since the dawn of man. Our myths are filled with Ancient Heroes taking on these giant beasts. In more recent history we have turned them into reluctant heroes in some cases and vicious predators in another. An entire sub-genre of film has sprung up around these colossal movie Monsters. The more extreme they grow in size, the better to freak out an audience.

You'd think that Giant Monsters in the real world would be easy to track because of their size, but there's a reason we don't hear more about these animals in the press.[2] They are even more adept at hiding than the rest of the Monsters we've already discussed, choosing to live in some of the most remote locations in the world. This is what has kept many of the creatures alive long past the time that others of their kind had become extinct. Just because they are big, does not mean they are easy to find.

Tracking Monsters is a key component in any Monster Hunter's job. This, of course, requires different skills for different Monsters. But, whether you are searching for a thundering Dinosaur or the illusive Unicorn, there are certain techniques that are universal for any Monster Hunter's needs.

1.   See: Zombies.
2.   Aside from the media blackout to avoid causing mass panic.

Hunters must also gather information.

In a perfect world, a Monster Hunter receives a call about a small pack of werewolves terrorizing a small town. The pack always attacks on the night of the full moon, enters the town from the same approach and retreats to the same part of the forest. The town is conveniently down the road from the Hunter's base of operations and the next full moon is over two weeks away, allowing plenty of time to prepare, pack the necessary equipment, study the area, and set up for the next attack.

Needless to say, we do not live in a perfect world. In most cases, the call you receive will be barely intelligible consisting of a lot of screaming before the line goes dead. You'll hop the next plane to some godforsaken part of the world and be on the case before your rented jeep even reaches the town limits. And, already, the locals will be complaining that you're too late to do any good. I've already discussed the importance on bringing the proper equipment.[3] Now it is time to reveal what to do once you get to the location.

Gathering evidence is the key to any good Hunt. Even when you know the type of creature you are dealing with, it is equally important to understand that being's motivations and behavior.

Witness interviews are both the most useful and least reliable methods of bringing yourself up to speed. Remember that you are often speaking with people following the most traumatic event of their lives. Imaginations can run wild. Some basic psychology classes as well as trauma training can teach you techniques for eliciting information from hysterical people. And even then, only trust about half of what you hear. For this reason, I usually hold off on any interviews until after I have examined the scene of the attack (or attacks) and have drawn my own conclusions.

Attack scenes should be approached with the same laser sharp focus of any traditional crime scene investigation. Cordon off the area if possible. Start with any kill spot and work your way out. Where traditional investigators are looking for physical clues, you must keep your mind open to other possibilities. The most horrific death scene I ever witnessed did not net one single physical clue to the identity of the killer Ghost.

3.   See Cryptids.

There are methods to Monster madness.

As Monster Hunters deal with a variety of quarry it is impossible to name one particular method as best for tracking subjects. The way we trail a Yeti is very different from how we hunt a Ghost. However, there are some basic techniques that can be used for all.

In investigating any attack or tracking any Monster, the first methods to be employed should be the most obvious. Traditional hunting techniques are the cornerstone of our business. I personally have trained with big game hunters, Native Americans, and ninjas to learn the best way to stealthily stalk real world prey. This type of tracking relies on the five natural senses of sight, scent, hearing, touch, and to a lesser degree, taste.[4]

Avoid using perfumes or heavily fragranced soaps. Not only on the day of the hunt, but for life in general. In many cases, it might be best not to bathe altogether on the morning of a Hunt to avoid unnatural scents. Never forget that while you Hunt, you are being Hunted as well.

Start by checking for all obvious signs of the direction the creature moved after an attack. A blood trail is often the easiest to follow. Again, this is where the knowledge of your Monster will come in most handy. Vampires do not tend to leave much destruction in their wake. The same cannot be said for Werewolves. You must remain alert during the tracking so that you do not become the next victim.

In addition to natural tracking techniques, there are supernatural methods that are easy for any layman to follow. Certain crystals, basic magic spells, and divining rods can be wielded by a novice to seek out paranormal disturbances.

Stealth is as important in Monster hunting as it is in traditional hunting. Use natural cover and camouflage of the area to blend into your surroundings. Unlike game hunters, we don't need silly orange vests to protect ourselves from other Hunters. It's exceedingly rare for two Monster Hunters to be working the same case separately. And even then, only a dolt would mistake another hunter for an actual Monster.

4.   I, for one, have no interest in tasting anything associated with a Zombie.

Megalodon

Origin: Natural
Locale: South Pacific
Effective Weaponry:
Torpedoes
Ineffective Weaponry:
Harpoons
Best Time to Hunt:
Dawn or Dusk
Worst Time to Hunt:
Night
Threat Level: Low

A Giant Shark from prehistoric times that hunts large prey in the South Pacific.

Why Megalodon, what big teeth you have.

The Giant Shark known as the Megalodon is one of many prehistoric Monsters believed to be extinct that you might run into in your travels. The name Megalodon means "Big Tooth" in Greek, due to the main evidence we have of the creature's existence. Most ancient and modern sharks constantly shed their teeth and grow replacements. Some fossilized teeth running up to seven inches in length have been found around the world dating back over a million years. These teeth are similar to that of the Great White Shark, though more formidable and the serration on the edging is more evenly distributed.

As shark bodies are mostly composed of cartilage and tissue it is extremely rare to find an intact fossil beyond that of the shark's teeth. As such, it is nearly impossible to get a true read on the size of the Megalodon based on fossil records. Among most, it is agreed to be approximately sixty to eighty feet in length with a mass of almost fifty tons. Some believe that the Megalodon died out a little over a million years ago, but teeth dating back only 11,000 years have been found. But what does this mean for the Monster Hunter of today? Is the Megalodon a current threat?

The answer to that question is something that I will rarely say: I do not know.

I personally have never encountered this magnificently terrifying beast, but I have collected enough eyewitness accounts to believe that the reports of its extinction have been greatly exaggerated. The creature seems to still live and create carnage in the South Pacific. The most notable sighting occurred in 1918 by fishermen off the coast of Broughton Island, Australia. Though skeptics believe this to be just one of many fish tales, I suspect that the opposite is true as reports of its existence continue to today.

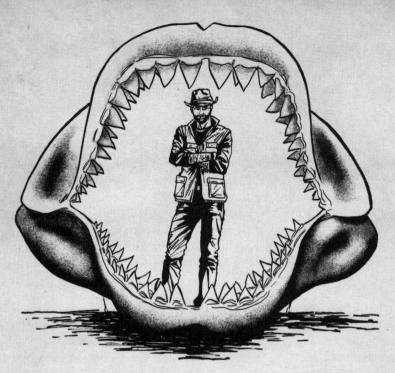

The Megalodon bites off considerably more than it chews.

There is no explanation for why such a large creature said to live off the coastline of Australia is so rarely seen. Some reports suggest that the lone Monster quietly existed for millennia in the deepest seas and only rose to the surface following some natural or manmade disturbance on the sea floor. This is likely not the case as the Megalodon is presumed to require warm water environments and could not survive the chilled waters of the lower depths. More likely is that the creature is a solitary being that has chosen hunting grounds away from humans, which are really too small of prey for it to desire.

The oversized teeth of the Megalodon are just the tip of this particular iceberg. Based on the size of those teeth, archaeologists have been able to reconstruct the creature's jaw to determine that the Monster could open its mouth six feet wide and seven feet high. With an estimated ten tons of biting force, the Megalodon has one of the most powerful bites of any creature in history. It can easily crack the shell of a giant tortoise and take on even the largest prey.

Its diet consists of larger marine animals, including whales. This carnivore is not selective, however. It will consume any size marine animal. In the 1918 sighting off Broughton Island, it reportedly devoured crayfish pots measuring three feet long, eating the contents and the wood and rope mesh pots themselves. In spite of the fact that there are no reported attacks on humans, I find it hard to believe that it has never made one of us its prey. Far more likely is that the creature has simply left no survivors.

The Megalodon's most fascinating attribute is that it changes its method of hunting based on the size of its prey. Preferring larger victims, it is believed to ram its prey from below, wounding it at the start of the attack. There is also evidence that the shark would sheer off its enemy's fins, rendering it unable to swim off. Like most sharks, the Megalodon is suspected to have multiple rows of teeth with the front set inflicting the most damage when it goes in for the kill. Once it takes off a hefty bite of its victim, it swallows the chunks of meat, without pausing to chew. There is little doubt that it could easily swallow a human victim whole.

Taking into consideration the size of the beast and the strength of its bite, avoid using smaller submersible vessels as they may not stand a chance against the Megalodon. It is believed that the sharkskin is incredibly durable, so an external attack it unlikely to produce effective results. I suspect that even the sharpest harpoon would bounce off the animal without it even noticing.

The best shot would be aiming a torpedo straight into the mouth of the shark and right down into the gullet, taking it out from the inside. This would be an incredibly risky venture, requiring the Monster Hunter to come within dining distance of the shark. Be aware that it is believed to be a very fast swimmer. Target practice is highly recommended as your aim will need to be true. You will likely get only one shot.

Giant Piranha

If we're going to open with the largest of sharks in existence, it's only logical to follow up with another fish that has bite: the Giant Piranha.

Piranhas don't have the best reputation and most of that is unearned. While it is true that Piranhas are carnivores, they generally feast on dead animals. On rare occasions, they have gone after live animal prey, but hardly ever attack a human. Unlike the media might have you believe, they do not hunt en masse and strip a human of flesh in seconds. These fish, averaging six to ten inches in length, aren't truly much of a threat.

The Giant Piranha, however, is a beast that is worth our attention. Also known as the Goliath Tigerfish, the carnivorous fish found in the Congo River can grow up to five feet long and weigh nearly one hundred pounds. Its thirty-two razor sharp teeth are each an average of three inches long and can pierce flesh and bone. It is among the most dangerous freshwater fish in the world, able to take chunks out of crocodiles as it does not hesitate to attack prey as large as itself.

That's just the public face of this river predator based on the media's insistence on presenting this rare creature as a negligible threat. But I have come face to tooth with this fearsome Monster and know that the truth is much worse.

The true Giant Piranha is ultra-aggressive, taking on prey considerably larger than its five foot body. This Piranha has been known to overturn boats on the Congo, making a quick meal out of the fishermen or explorers in it. Think of it as the most aggressive shark you'll ever meet in a river.

Conveniently, the Giant Piranha is very little challenge for a fully trained Monster Hunter. Taking one on is quite similar to catching the average shark. The danger of this creature merely comes from being unprepared to meet it. Smaller fishing boats will easily fall to its strength in the water. You'll need a vessel with some size to it to withstand a blow from the fish, which is the predator's typical initial attack move.

Of course, no simple lure or worm will be enough to tempt the Giant Piranha your way. You'll need to chum the water as you would with a shark. However, these Monsters have more sophisticated tastes. Their interest in fish is limited. Bloody chunks of beef make for a far more irresistible treat. You're going to need an eighty pound line to reel the sucker in once you've got it. Usually this is a two person job. But again, make sure the person assisting you knows what he's doing. Getting too close to the fish as it thrashes is a welcome invitation to join it in the water. A club will be necessary to finish it off before you bring it into the boat as it is still a danger out of the water. Once the fish is incapacitated a standard hunting knife can finish the job, leaving you with a robust trophy for your wall.

Giant Octopus

The Giant Octopus, while smaller than its distant cousin, the Kraken, is still a considerable threat. It is one of the most intelligent of the Giant Monsters you will encounter, employing stealth and a variety of defensive tricks in its attack.

There is only one record of a beached Giant Octopus, though the media (through government intervention) has most of the world population convinced that it was actually the carcass of a sperm whale. The body of that Giant Octopus was twenty-three feet long with tentacles averaging thirty feet in length. In my experience, this was a smaller version of these Giants. I personally have seen Octopuses with tentacles stretching seventy-five feet.[5]

Similar to the Kraken, the Giant Octopus will ensnare a boat in its tentacles, clamping on with the suckers that run the length of its limbs. Though it does not have the strength of the Kraken and cannot pose a threat to larger ships, the Giant Octopus can do damage to the average pleasure cruiser by plucking individual victims from the deck and feeding them into its beak that lies in the center of its arms. It also possesses venom that will paralyze its victims before it goes in for the kill.

When hunting, the Giant Octopus shoots ink from ink sacs to murk the waters and mask its approach. It is also a master of camouflage and often lies in wait for unsuspecting scuba divers to get too close.

Taking on a Giant Octopus is good practice for the Kraken as they are a challenge to combat, but not nearly as impossible to kill. Small explosives should be enough to do the trick. Bladed weapons are sometimes strong enough to sever the limbs until you can get close enough to deliver a killing blow.

5.   Mind you, this is an estimate. It's not like I was whipping out a tape measure at the time.

Another sea creature sometimes mistaken for the Kraken is the Giant Squid. Reports of this beast had been mostly kept under wraps until a Japanese research team caught evidence of it on film in 2004. They recorded a Squid that was approximately twenty-six feet long that probably looked quite terrifying to the average civilian. What few people realize is that it was just a baby.

The Giant Squid has been a major player in the stories of ancient mariners throughout the centuries. It has left its battle scars on the whales that comprise its main enemy under the seas. It is more feared than the Giant Octopus, but only by a matter of degrees. Using the sharp hooks in its tentacles, the Giant Squid can latch onto most sea going vessels, tearing apart the rubber coating on the hull of a frigate. Now imagine what those tentacles can do to a person and you understand the viciousness of the attack.

The Giant Squid lives in depths so deep that it is nearly impossible for light to penetrate the darkness. Taking on Monsters in their natural habitat is rarely wise to begin with, but it is impossible to search out this creature in the depths where it makes its home. Better to wait for it to surface when feeding. You just have to hope you can get there before it kills too many people.

Considering that squid have the largest eyes in the animal kingdom, that's the place to focus your attack. A couple harpoons to the eyes will blind the squid, putting it in so much pain that it will release whatever it holds. Mind you, it lives in the dark, so just because you've blinded it doesn't mean you've removed its ability to track you. The Squid relies on other senses to take out its prey. You must move fast, while it is in pain to finish it off with an explosive device or depth charge.

Roc

Origin: Natural
Locale: South China Sea
Effective Weaponry: Missiles
Ineffective Weaponry: Guns
Best Time to Hunt: Midday
Worst Time to Hunt: Night
Threat Level: High

An enormous bird that lives up to the fantastic tales surrounding its existence.

Many myths begin with fact.

Earlier[6] we looked at the myths surrounding the Thunderbird and separated the exaggerated fiction from the facts of the Avian Monster. Unfortunately, that's not so easy to do with the Roc as many of the myths surrounding this Giant Bird are true. In fact, some believe that the Roc was the genesis of the mythical aspects of the Thunderbird.

As with many of the Giant Monsters you might encounter, the Roc is an incredibly rare beast. This shouldn't come as much of a surprise since flocks of birds the size of jetliners would cause the media to be flooded with sightings. I don't care how big the world is, there's simply not enough airspace to hide something this large.

Stories of the Roc date back centuries, in which the creature went by many names, including the variants Rukh, Ruc, and Rukhkh. The Giant Bird figures prominently in the Middle Eastern folk tales collected in One Thousand and One Nights[7] and Marco Polo's book of travels. Kubla Khan once reportedly sent men out in search of the giant beast. They returned with an enormous feather as evidence of its existence, though skeptics claim it was merely a frond from the Raphia palm.

6.   In the previous section on Cryptids.
7.   Better known as 1001 Arabian Nights.

Just because it's big and scary, doesn't mean it's good in a fight.

In addition to its massive size, the Roc is also known for possessing enormous strength. It preys on larger animals and can easily lift an elephant. The Roc's main method of feeding is to lift its quarry into the air and drop it from a great height, killing it on impact. The Roc then lands and feeds on the remains. As a result, the Roc isn't much of a fighter since its size and the advantage of flight allows it to easily subdue most of its victims.

The average human is considered too insignificant for the Roc to concern itself with, preferring larger prey such as rhinoceroses, hippopotamuses, and the aforementioned elephant. That's not to say that it will not attack a human when in the mood for a light snack, but it is unlikely. One of the tales of Sinbad even speaks of how the sailor lashed himself to a Roc's legs to use the creature as a method of escape and went totally unnoticed. I have my doubts about this tale as the Roc is not the type of beast to allow anyone or anything to sneak up on it.

It's far more likely that another tale from 1001 Nights is true, however. This one recounts the events that followed when the crew of a ship feasted on a newly hatched baby Roc. The mother attacked the ship by picking up giant boulders and dropping them on the ship, demolishing it and killing much of the crew in the process.

Stories of the Roc have spread across Asia and the Middle East, but Roc nests are almost exclusively found on islands in the South China Sea. Or, more to the point, Roc nests are islands in the South China Sea. There are many stories of innocent travelers stopping to explore an island only to find out the hard way that they've stumbled into a Roc nest. Usually they can escape unscathed, unless there are eggs or recent hatchlings in the nest. Luckily, Rocs rarely procreate or else these giants would overrun us.

The unfortunate reality of hunting a Roc is that you will need heavy weaponry. The preferred method is to sneak onto its nest and leave a massive amount of explosives that will destroy the Monster and its nest. This is a particularly risky maneuver since there is no guarantee that the bird won't fly off in the time it takes you to clear the blast radius. The only way to ensure that would be through a suicide mission, blowing the island nest while you are still within range of the bird and the blast. This is, of course, a fool's errand, that only a Hunter wanting to make a name for himself would do. I speak from experience having witnessed one of my apprentices do just that. Stupid, yes. But I can honestly say that I will never forget what's his name.

The most expedient way to take out this beast requires a fighter jet loaded with missiles. As there are no avian predators larger than the Roc, it is entirely unfamiliar with defending itself against an attack from the air simply because it has no experience with air combat. Just be aware that a single flap of a Roc's wings is enough to disrupt air currents, so it is best not to get too close to the creature. For the less adventurous Hunter,[8] I recommend surface to air missiles. What it lacks in excitement, it certainly makes up for with effectiveness. Of course, fighter jets and missiles are generally outside a Monster Hunter's budget. You also run the risk of starting an international incident by crossing into Chinese airspace, but those are more concerns for politicians. You've got a battle to fight.

8.   As if there is such a thing.

Giant Spider

Origin: Natural
Locale: Caves
Effective Weaponry:
Shotgun, Bladed
Weapons, Flamethrower
Best Time to Hunt:
Day
Worst Time to Hunt:
Night
Threat Level: Moderate

A massive, eight-legged arachnid that has inspired nightmares all around the globe.

Spider combat is a family affair.

Few things strike fear into the hearts of everyday civilians like the sight of a tiny little spider crawling up the wall. Now imagine that fear multiplied one hundred times and you can understand the mass panic caused by the mere idea of a Giant Spider attack. Luckily, this colossal arachnid rarely ventures into populated areas, preferring to weave its webs deep in the darkest forests and caves on every continent of the world except Antarctica. In the unlikely event that one of these Monsters ventures into a city, be ready to call out the National Guard to deal with the ensuing hysteria.

Monster Hunters have received more and more calls about Giant Spiders as populations have grown and encroached on their territory. It's unfortunate that these creatures have become among our top hunted Monsters through no fault of their own. Yet relocating them has been ruled out as an option as they are fiercely predatory and almost impossible to ensnare due to the large number of offspring that populate the nest.

A fully grown Giant Spider has a body about the size of a VW Van, though I would not suggest driving one of those fine vehicles up to the creature to take it on. The van will not survive the encounter.[9] Conveniently, you'll only come across one full grown Giant Spider in every nest. It's the children of that Spider you need to most concern yourself with. On average, they are more the size of an ottoman with legs. Still big, but not nearly as fearsome.

The mother Spider lays hundreds of eggs at a time, but these ultra-aggressive offspring are forever killing each other off until one of them becomes the new head of household when the mother dies. This happens over a period of decades and usually keeps them quite entertained and away from humans. On rare occasions, one of the offspring will make its way out into the world to form a new nest, which is when we receive the panicked phone calls for a massive extermination project.

9.   Neither will the idiotic apprentice so stupid as to think that a mint condition mint green
        VW Vanagon carefully restored by its actual owner is a proper attack vehicle for this kind of hunt!

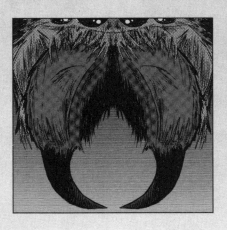

Always go for the leader before the soldiers.

Giant Spiders are among the most predatory Monsters you will encounter. They employ several methods of attack and kill indiscriminately. I'm sure that I don't need to describe a Giant Spider to you, but just in case, we'll start with the basics. Like their tiny counterparts, these arachnids have eight legs on a body segmented by head and abdomen. The retractable fangs sitting beneath the multiple eyes in their face, inject their victims with poisonous venom that paralyzes on contact, but is very slow to actually kill. It is imperative that you do not get too close to the creature's face. Coming at it from behind is equally unadvisable as their spinnerets produce a thick adhesive silk that entraps their victims.

The Giant Spider employs several attack methods. The predominant tactic is to lure their prey into their web. It is not unusual for a person to stumble all the way into a Spider nest unscathed and totally unaware that every footstep is being watched by thousands of eyes. Once the victim is captured, the Giant Spider will inject the prey with its venom and weave its silk around the body, encasing it for feeding. Since Spiders do not have traditional mouths, they can only ingest liquefied foods. As the victim dies the slow agonizing death, the Spider will pump digestive fluid into the body and suck the liquefied guts out of the body. God willing you will be dead before that process begins.

When a simple lure is not enough to get its victims into the web, the Spider and its offspring will use a more aggressive method of outflanking the victim and forcing it into the web. That's why it's important to always keep an eye out in front of you when being chased by a Spider. You are almost certainly being herded into a trap. Of course, it's always possible that the Spider is merely running you down and will pounce, shooting out its silk to trap you and then dragging you off to die.

Our focus on dealing with the Giant Spider will be on the largest of the species, namely: the mother Spider. Once that beast is killed the frenzy among its offspring to take its place usually takes out the bulk of the nest on its own. The Monster Hunter's main concern is just getting past the smaller Giants to the mamma. Conveniently, as part of their predatory behavior, they will usually let you slip right by so long as they believe you are falling into their trap and not the other way around.

As Giant Spiders spend much of their time in dark caves, their vision is rather acute. You should always carry a pair of night vision goggles as well as a powerful flashlight and/or flares to blind them if necessary. Be aware that their main source of determining a victim is approaching is through vibrations so take gentle steps if possible.

Unlike the gossamer silk produced by their tiny cousins, the Giant Spider's webbing is nearly impossible to break with your bare hands. Always carry several knives on your person. I suggest at least one in an ankle holster, one at your waist, and a third wrist ejector blade as you never know what will be the easiest to grasp if you are caught up in the web.

Taking out the Spider's legs will slow it down, but do little damage. The only surefire attack on a Spider is from above, which is usually quite difficult in a cave. If possible, lure it out into the trees where you can come at it from the branches. A blade to the cephalothorax (head) will take out the brain while piercing the top of the opisthosoma (abdomen) will destroy the heart. At that point, any smaller Spiders will almost surely forget that you are there as they begin their battle for supremacy. Always be sure to burn the Spider's corpse as eggs inside the mother can still hatch after death and you do not want to have to come back to deal with future offspring. With that done, you can take care of the surviving Spiders, eradicating the entire nest for good.

Sucuriju Gigante

Origin: Natural
Locale: Amazon River
Effective Weaponry:
Explosives
Ineffective Weaponry:
Machete
Best Time to Hunt:
Day
Worst Time to Hunt:
Night
Threat Level: Moderate

The proper name for the Giant Anaconda that is known throughout South America.

Monster Hunting should only be carried out by trained professionals.

The Sucuriju Gigante, or Giant Anaconda, is one of the most well known of the Giant Monsters that a Monster Hunter will encounter. Reports of the Giant Anaconda stretch back to the time the South American continent was "discovered" by European explorers though it is mentioned in native folklore that long predate that time period. The oversized snake is also known as the "Bull Eater" and is a formidable opponent for any Monster Hunter.

According to official records, the largest Anaconda ever found was only twenty-eight feet in length. That's nothing compared to the size of Sucuriju Gigante. I've personally seen snakes of this variety stretching out to well over one hundred feet and close to a yard in circumference.[10] Reportedly, they can weigh up to five tons, though I've never attempted to weigh one. I can say that it is impossible to drag its dead carcass out of the water on your own and usually requires several highly paid workers to do the job for you.

The Giant Anaconda is believed to be a descendant of the Gigantophis Snake of the Eocene period. Or, as with many of these creatures, it is an actual survivor from that time. To my knowledge, no one has recorded the true age of this Monster as its body rarely remains intact long enough for a proper examination.[11]

This snake has been a highly valued prize since its first witnessed reports. President Theodore Roosevelt even placed a $50,000 bounty on the creature, hoping to bring the skin of the Giant Anaconda to the Bronx zoo. The prize was never collected and several lives were lost in the process.

10.   And I, personally, was the last thing those snakes ever saw.
11.   More on that in a moment.

Sometimes the eyes aren't nearly as big as the stomach.

There have been reports of oversized water snakes in tropical climates all over the world, but the prime hunting ground for the Sucuriju Gigante is in the Amazon Rainforest of South America. I've found that the easiest place to find these snakes is along the Rio Negro River, but the giant beast has capsized and crushed boats in almost every waterway in the Amazon. It has been known to wind its huge body around smaller fishing boats, crushing them and sending the occupants into the water where it finishes them off.

The preferred method of attack for a Giant Anaconda is a head on confrontation. Unlike a traditionally sized anaconda, the Sucuriju Gigante has lightning fast reflexes and can pounce in the blink of an eye. It coils itself around its prey, crushing it in a tight embrace powerful enough to kill a bull. The average human has no chance once the coils are around him. Luckily, the power of this massive beast is such that death generally comes quickly. The Anaconda does not play with its food.

Once its victim is trapped within its coils, the jaw of the Giant Anaconda unhinges, allowing it to swallow even the largest prey whole. The beast has teeth, but it rarely uses them as part of its attack. If anything, the teeth are merely a means for holding onto the prey while the coils wrap around the body. This snake is not venomous, but that really doesn't matter as its sharp teeth are enough to cause a deadly injury on their own.

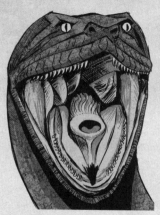

Just because your prey is big, doesn't mean it can't hide.

Even at its massive size, the Giant Anaconda has impressive camouflage abilities, easily blending into the rainforest surroundings making it incredibly difficult to hunt. When it is swimming, part of the long body remains hidden in the water, so it is often difficult to get a true estimation of what you are dealing with until it is almost upon you. There's a considerable difference between taking on a regular anaconda and his giant brethren. A machete isn't going to cut it for the Sucuriju Gigante, though it doesn't hurt to be armed with one to defend against smaller snakes.

The Sucuriju Gigante is a difficult Monster to hunt because your best shot at it will be in the water. As with most Giant Monsters, explosives should be your weapon of choice. Bullets will not pierce the thick snakeskin and even the sharpest blades can't get deep enough into the creature to do any real harm. Although, one time I did have some success using the propeller of a larger fishing boat in much the way I did with a Sea Serpent. My preferred method of hunting is to lure the creature to me by dropping a larger animal into the river. Anacondas prefer live bait, so a slab of meat from the butcher will net you nothing.

I've found it best to dispose of the snake's body immediately, lest you attract unwanted predators. I'm speaking, of course, of human predators who feel like they have any right to come in once the job is done and claim the prize as their own. The meat of the Sucuriju Gigante is a true delicacy that can fetch an exceedingly high price on the open market and is a good way for a Monster Hunter to supplement his income.

Giant Alligator

It's one of the most popular urban legends ever told, but by now I hope it doesn't come as a surprise to learn that this story is actually true. There really are Alligators in the sewers of New York.[12] They've been there as early as the 1930s, reaching the height of their infestation in the sixties and continuing on today.

Vacationing parents in the golden days of stupidity used to bring baby alligators home from Florida for their kids without possessing enough foresight to realize that baby alligators become actual full-grown adult alligators. Once the little biters grew to be too much for the family aquarium, they would be foolishly flushed down the toilet to get rid of the problem … only to create a brand new one.

By all rights, these helpless creatures should have died in the cold darkness beneath the city as Alligators are cold blooded and require warmer climates to survive. What no one could have suspected was that the mix of chemicals found in the typical waste of the average New Yorker would have an unexpected effect on them. The Alligators mutated to thrive in even the coldest city winters and grew to a size that surpassed that of the largest recorded alligator in the Everglades.

The New York City government has engaged in an aggressive media campaign to downplay the problem of the giant predatory alligators that make their home in the city's sewers. They've even gone so far as to create a shadow group of sewer workers off the books specifically trained for encounters with these giant creatures deep in the bowels of the underground. The fact that you rarely hear of the dozens of city workers that lose their lives every year to these Monsters is a testament to the cover up.

12.   In other cities as well, but this is predominantly a New York phenomenon.

The habitat of the Giant Alligator makes Hunting a challenge, but fighting a breeze. There are hundreds of miles of sewer beneath the city of New York dropping down multiple levels beneath the streets. The newer, smaller tunnels directly under the surface are relatively safe as they've been designed to be inaccessible to these giant predators. When Alligator evidence is found near the safe areas, that section is closed off, effectively trapping the Alligator.

It's difficult to track an Alligator in the lower sewers as the miles and miles of sewer tunnels double back on themselves with twists and turns in the most unlikely junctions. Alligators feed off the rats that are plentiful at these depths, but hardly ever leave any evidence of their kill behind. The groundwater at this level also washes away much of their tracks. Conveniently, these Alligators are always hungry and your scent will naturally draw them to you.

Once the Monster is found, battling in this environment is surprisingly easy. The unnatural size of the Alligator works against it as it is often has to squeeze through the tunnels, rendering the rear half of its body—including the dangerous tail—entirely ineffective. A high-powered shotgun or assault rifle should do the trick,[13] however you must aim into the Alligator's open maw to get to the soft fleshy inside since the exterior is particularly hard. Not to worry since the Alligator will always open its mouth as it bears down on you. Do not hesitate with your shot or I shouldn't need to tell you what will happen.

The true danger occurs if the Alligator ever gets topside and is no longer contained to the tunnels. When it has a freer range of movement and can lash out with its tail, your challenge increases tenfold. In that case, you're going to want heavier artillery allowing you to remain at a safe distance. I've found that a bazooka is a useful weapon for this task. Just be careful of the fleeing people and causing excessive property damage. The City of New York is one of the most likely of any local government to charge you for the damage you cause ridding them of their problem.

13.   Explosives are not recommended. You don't want to bring the sewer down around you.

Dinosaurs

Origin: Natural
Locale: Global?
Effective Weaponry: ??
Ineffective Weaponry: ??
Best Time to Hunt: ??
Worst Time to Hunt: ??
Threat Level: ???

The Giant Lizards that roamed the Earth long before humans. Dinosaurs supposedly died out in a massive extinction event sixty-five million years ago, but evidence has shown that some may have survived.

Dinosaurs still roam the Earth … and not in some theme park ride gone amuck, either. They are all around us in the form of their descendants and the actual immortal dinosaurs themselves. Whether we call them Nessie, or Megalodon, or Mokele-mbembe, it is clear that these "Terrible Lizards" have been around for a while. "New" Monster species are always being rediscovered, so it is best to familiarize yourself will all manner of Dinosaur just in case you stumble across one in your travels. The following are three of the most dangerous Dinosaurs that ever lived. Though I have no evidence that they are still around,[14] I suggest keeping an eye out for them in your travels, lest they get an eyeful of you first.

Tyrannosaurus Rex: Known as the King of the Dinosaurs, this nearly ten ton beast with sharp teeth is believed to be one of the most feared predators ever born.

Utahraptor: Among the most dangerous of the raptor family, what this Dinosaur lacked in the speed of its cousins, it made up for in sheer brute strength.

Allosaurus: Though believed to be lacking in intelligence, the high number of full grown Dinosaur fossils found indicates that this was one of the most abundant of Giant Lizards to have lived, suggesting that it was the top of the food chain.

14.   And, man, I would love it if they were.

Mokele-mbembe

One Dinosaur that we do know of currently living in the forests and swamps of the Congo in Central Africa goes by the name Mokele-mbembe. This Sauropod was incorrectly believed to have become extinct with the other Dinosaurs over sixty-five million years ago, though no scientist can explain how it survived.

The name, Mokele-mbembe, comes from the Lingala language and means "one that stops the flow of rivers." At over thirty feet long and weighing several tons, this is an apt description of the reddish-brown skinned dinosaur. Some reports have it rising to seventy-five feet in height from foot to head. Most sightings confirm that the creature's neck stretches from five to ten feet from its body, which is enough height to allow it to reach the leaves of trees along the riverbank. The relatively small head of this lizard is topped by a frill crest, similar to that found on a rooster.

On the opposite end is a tail that stretches out five feet behind it. The

dinosaur's thick, elephantine legs end in rounded, feet that measure approximately three feet in diameter and have three clawed toes.

Mokele-mbembe is an herbavore known to feed off the leaves on treetops as well as aquatic vegetation, primarily the Malombo plant. But do not be fooled into believing that its vegetarian diet makes it less of a threat. The Mokele-mbembe is an aggressive animal when it believes its territory is threatened. It has flipped over boats and killed explorers with its tail or its vicious bite. The Dinosaur never feeds on these victims, though. This is merely how it protects itself.

Numerous expeditions have gone in search of Mokele-mbembe, but few have returned with evidence of its existence. Fewer still have returned at all. This is the folly of explorers who have tried to disturb a creature that values its privacy and aggressively defends its territory.

Your search for the Mokele-mbembe must take a different approach than a traditional Hunt. I believe that it should be a Monster Hunter's goal to protect this dinosaur from trespassers, while protecting the trespassers from themselves. When left to its own devices, the Mokele-mbembe is a docile creature. It is the human interlopers that cause it to become threatening.

As such, I have taken on the cause of protecting the Mokele-mbembe. Unfortunately, this is not as simple as relocating the Dinosaur.[15] The Giant Lizard cannot differentiate between a human out to protect it versus one that wants to do it harm. And, quite frankly, why should it be moved from the land that has provided safe refuge to it and its ancestors for millions of years? This is one of the oldest Monsters on the planet and it certainly has more right to this little patch of the Congo than we do.

Conveniently, most Mokele-mbembes are content to live out their lives in a relatively small plot of the swamp. Rather than taking them to a preserve, I have set up a standard operating procedure for turning their homes into preserves. Once set up, with proper signage posted to warn off big game hunters, these safe zones should keep the dinosaurs safe for as long as I am doing my job.

15.   Contrary to how I believe relocating Bigfoot Creatures is better for their protection.

The bigger they are, the truly harder they do fall.

Giant Monsters are the big, big brothers in the Cryptid family. They aren't just the things that go bump in the night. They also go boom, bang, and smash. They make for an interesting contrast of being so large, yet so difficult for the average person to find, which is just as well since the average person wouldn't have a clue what to do if he stumbled across one of them.

Having discussed the creatures of the natural world over the past two sections, our Cryptozoological studies now move into a more supernatural realm. We will next explore the Monsters that may visually resemble the animals that we hunt on the jungles and plains, but have much more of a mystical explanation for their existence. From here we move on to examine the Unnatural Beasts…

UNNATURAL BEASTS

There's a thin line between natural and unnatural.

In exploring Cryptozoology we dealt largely with Monsters of the natural world; the quirks of evolution that may be rare, but still somewhat mesh with our understanding of how the animal kingdom functions. But the term "Monster" is far-reaching in its definition. It covers a whole host of beings that either evolved along with humans or came to exist through otherworldly means.

Unnatural Beasts are the result of a magical influence on evolution. Monsters like Vampires and Zombies may have as much science behind their origins as mysticism, but as I've said before, magic is most certainly real. It is responsible for the cursed creatures that roam our world with a little extra darkness in their souls. Oftentimes these savages mix natural abilities with supernatural to provide even greater challenges for the Monster Hunter. It's not enough to fire a bullet at your prey, it has to be a silver bullet to properly do the deed.[1]

Unlike Ghosts or Ghouls, many of these Unnatural Beasts can be mistaken for the animals of the natural world. This can be dangerous for any number of reasons, not the least of which being that you need to know how to defend yourself from what you come up against. Often you will have no more than a split second to determine the threat level of the pounding footsteps approaching through the forest.[2]

In many cases we don't know the true origin of the magic that made the first of their kind, but that isn't always necessary for us to do our jobs. The history that concerns us should be focused on the methods that have successfully killed them in the past. Where they came from can be an entertaining story, but it doesn't always have impact on our jobs.

Like their natural counterparts, Unnatural Beasts can be found all over the world in various locations, climates, and elevations. The proper Monster Hunter must be prepared to face evil wherever it may take you.

---

1.   Silver has both physical and metaphysical properties that make it an all around useful tool for Monster Hunters.
2.   If you can't spot the differences between a wolf and a Werewolf you're also going to have PETA on your ass.

Become a Monster Hunter. See the world.

Many fledgling Monster Hunters filled their heads with dreams of exotic destinations. I can understand why. My passport is stamped with locales most people never imagine visiting: Africa, South America, Australia, New Jersey. Monster Hunters rack up frequent flyer miles on a monthly basis. We take calls from every corner of the globe in languages familiar and completely foreign before jetting off to distant lands. It may seem glamorous, but that couldn't be further from the truth. We are not on vacation. We are on the Hunt.

Sightseeing takes a backseat to what we see in our gun sights when we arrive in these foreign cities and towns. And remember, it's mostly towns. Only the boldest of Monsters venture into populated areas these days. Usually you'll find yourself in some godforsaken backwater village that barely has electricity, much less an internet connection. Whether your destination is a major tourist attraction or a place that isn't even on a map there are universal tips to keep in mind when it comes to traveling for the Hunt.

Frequent Flyer miles are a must. Monster Hunting isn't exactly a high paying occupation. When I do get paid, I always charge for travel expenses. But these wonderful gift miles put a little extra cash in my pocket. Also, the upgrades are worth it. If you're flying to the other side of the Earth, why not treat yourself to an upgrade? You should be properly rested when it's time to face your enemy.

Invest in an alias (or two). Mind you, I'm not suggesting anyone do anything illegal. It's just that mistakes can happen in our business. An important landmark that is the source of much tourist revenue can accidentally be destroyed during a fight with a Dragon.[3] Not every government wants us back after we've rid them of their problem. In some cases, having an alternate identity can speed the process of reentry into a country.

3.   This should not be taken as an admission for any damage some people may claim I've caused.

Getting there is half the work.

Planes can only take you so far in this world. But getting from the airport to the more isolated areas of attack can present as many challenges as Monster Combat. When possible, try to make all travel arrangements before you leave home. Failing that, you should learn how to quickly identify potential allies upon arriving in a foreign land. You're going to need a trustworthy guide that can get you in and out of the fray, not a scammer only interested in bilking you out of your money.

Know the locals and the locales. Yes, you've been invited to most Monster infestations, but the local population is already on edge by the time you arrive. You may be their savior, but you're also a stranger entering a very strange situation. Familiarize yourself with local customs before you arrive at your destination. Make your presence known to the town leaders so they can ease your acceptance among their people. This is also useful for determining who will be paying you when the job is done.[4]

Learn the language: Screaming in terror is fairly universal, but there are some key words and phrases that are more useful to know. I don't expect Monster Hunters to be fluent in every language on the planet. We have more important things to learn. But I do recommend committing the following phrases to memory in at least a dozen different languages to get you through most encounters:

- Tell me what happened.
- Did it have fangs/claws/tentacles?
- Where was it last seen?
- Where is the nearest hospital?
- Call for reinforcements.
- Get down.
- Help.

Take some time to see the sights. Unless you've been run out of town, it doesn't hurt to stick around to make sure the job has been properly completed and that the threat is truly gone. Besides, all work and no play makes a Monster Hunter a bitter old wretch. Build some time into your trips so that once the Hunt is done, you can enjoy a night or two on the town in some of the more hopping destinations. Some kinds of trouble you might enjoy getting into.

4.   I suggest always getting at least half your fee up front.

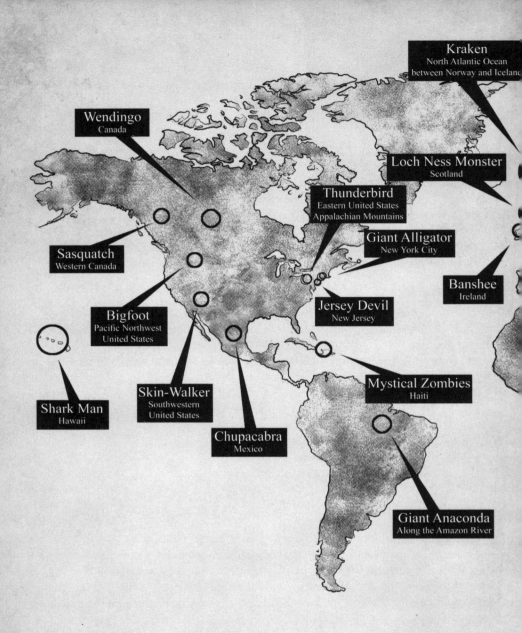

Kraken
North Atlantic Ocean
between Norway and Iceland

Wendingo
Canada

Loch Ness Monster
Scotland

Thunderbird
Eastern United States
Appalachian Mountains

Giant Alligator
New York City

Sasquatch
Western Canada

Banshee
Ireland

Bigfoot
Pacific Northwest
United States

Jersey Devil
New Jersey

Shark Man
Hawaii

Skin-Walker
Southwestern
United States

Mystical Zombies
Haiti

Chupacabra
Mexico

Giant Anaconda
Along the Amazon River

Monsters are found on every continent in the world, with the possible exception of Antarctica. Some, like Vampires, are a global threat haunting cities and towns across the map. Others gather in a particular region and make their home. The following locations list the highest concentrations of some of the Monster species we've discussed. This is by no means a complete list. Those creatures that exist worldwide have been excluded.

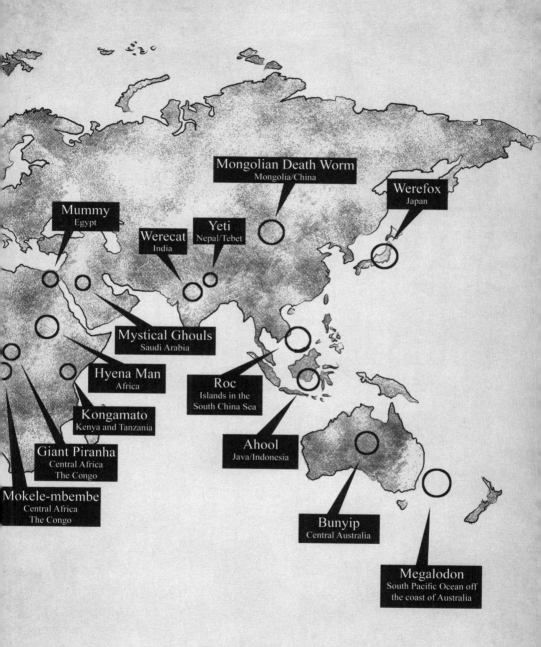

Mongolian Death Worm
Mongolia/China

Werefox
Japan

Mummy
Egypt

Werecat
India

Yeti
Nepal/Tebet

Mystical Ghouls
Saudi Arabia

Hyena Man
Africa

Roc
Islands in the
South China Sea

Kongamato
Kenya and Tanzania

Giant Piranha
Central Africa
The Congo

Ahool
Java/Indonesia

Mokele-mbembe
Central Africa
The Congo

Bunyip
Central Australia

Megalodon
South Pacific Ocean off
the coast of Australia

Chupacabra

Origin: Natural or Supernatural
Locale: Central America
Indentifying traits: Red, glowing eyes and coarse gray fur
Effective Weaponry: Guns
Ineffective Weaponry: Anything from Vampire mythology
Best Time to Hunt: Night
Worst Time to Hunt: Day
Threat Level: Moderate

Known as the "goat sucker," this Vampiric creature drains the blood of livestock, terrorizing farming communities in Central America.

Chupacabras will get your goat ... and any other animals you have.

Taking its name from the Spanish words chupar "to suck" and cabra "goat," the Chupacabra has earned a reputation for draining the lives of livestock in much the way Vampires drain humans. Don't let the name fool you, though. The Chupacabra stalks more than just goats. It has been known to attack prey ranging from chickens to horses and cattle more than twice its size. Although there has never been a recorded human attack, the highly aggressive Chupacabra hunts in sparsely populated areas away from major cities. It is entirely possible that any human victims may have simply gone unreported.

Tales of the Chupacabra harks back to Central American native myths about a so-called "mosquito man" that sucks the blood of animals through a long snout. Although these stories have been around for centuries, it was not until the mid-1990s that the Chupacabra shifted from legend to living Monster status. Since then, the creature has been found in most Latin American territories, although the highest concentration seems to be in Mexico and Puerto Rico. The first modern report of Chupacabra activity came in 1995 with the death of eight sheep drained entirely of their blood. This was actually a small kill since some of these Monsters have been responsible for the deaths of up to 150 livestock in one night.

A Chupacabra attack is fast and direct. It drains the blood—and sometimes organs—of its victims leaving behind two puncture wounds as evidence. Chupacabra fangs are quite large, leaving behind puncture wounds big enough to fit a human finger in. Some reports incorrectly cite that the Chupacabra uses its claws to feed on victims, leaving three puncture wounds in a triangular shape, but I have yet to see such a wound myself.

If it looks like a Vampire and acts like a Vampire, it isn't always a Vampire.

Descriptions of the Chupacabra vary wildly. It's been said to look like everything from a humanoid lizard with greenish skin to a small, hairy bear. It is one of the most consistently misidentified Monsters that you will Hunt. This is probably due to terror it strikes in its witnesses that leads to inaccurate reports. With behavior that mimics the Vampire, a certain level of fear from those who have seen it is understandable. But that's pretty much where the similarities end. It does not share any traits with the Vampire beyond the manner in which it feeds. In fact, we can't really confirm that it is an Unnatural Beast, as opposed to a traditional Cryptid. However, some of its powers do seem supernatural in origin, which is why I've classified it in this manner.

First, we should cut through the false sightings to report on the Chupacabra's true appearance. The beast stands roughly three-to-four feet tall when on its hind legs. It can travel upright on two feet or on all fours. The entire body is covered in coarse, gray hair. It has a dorsal ridge on its back, long teeth surrounding its extended fangs, claws, and a tail.

The Chupacabra is an incredibly fleet-footed animal. It moves with a swiftness that can easily outpace the average human when it travels on all fours. From an upright position, it can hop a distance of over twenty feet, enabling it to cross gullies and creeks with ease.

The supernatural aspect of the Chupacabra can be found in its glowing red eyes. The Chupacabra's stare has been known to nauseate humans and paralyze animal victims. Avoid the creature's gaze when in a fight as it will use this power to weaken you and either escape or attack.

Hunting the Chupacabra is a difficult task because of its attraction to remote areas, which allows it to move at full speed with few obstructions. Your best bet is to lure it out into the open with livestock. The distraction of a meal is sometimes enough to compensate for the heightened senses that could give away the approach of a human predator. Sightings of the creature have occurred almost exclusively at night, so that is when you should take on the Hunt. It is rarely seen in the daytime. To the best of my knowledge, a Chupacabra nest has never been found so we have no idea the type of habitat to search for while it is in its dormant state.

The Chupacabra has a sulfuric scent that is often the first indication of its approach. When alarmed, the creature will hiss and let out a distinctive screech unlike any sound I have heard in nature. Trust me when I say that once you hear this screech, you will never forget.

The Chupacabra's strongest weapon—its paralyzing eyes—is also its most easily exploited weakness. The creature shies away from bright, shiny light. A gun with a high-powered flashlight attachment will disorient the Chupacabra long enough for you to get off a clean shot before it can flee.

The Jersey Devil

Unlike the Chupacabra, which can go either way in the natural/unnatural debate, there is little question of the otherworldly origin of The Jersey Devil. Found almost exclusively in the Pine Barrens of New Jersey, this bipedal creature walks upright on hooves when it is not flying with its bat-like wings. It has two short front legs, a long neck, a head similar to a horse's and a forked tail. Reports on the Jersey Devil's height vary from four to eight feet, though consensus has placed it at just over six feet tall. Some sightings have made note of its glowing red eyes and the scream it emits that is similar to a shrill human cry.

Many call the Jersey Devil the very essence of evil. They consider it a harbinger of war that has terrorized the area for over three hundred years. Several versions of its origin story exist, but each one is clear in the satanic explanation behind its creation. My favorite of the stories tells of a woman with a dozen children. When she learned she was pregnant with her thirteenth child, she said in exasperation that the devil could have it. The devil took the offer seriously.

Moments after its birth the baby changed in front of its mother's eyes. Wings erupted from its back, hands and feet shifted into claws and hooves, and the rest of its body took on the form it now holds. The little Devil killed its family before flying out of the home to haunt the surrounding barrens to this day.

The Jersey Devil is credited with massive numbers of livestock deaths over the centuries and it has been known to attack humans. It's existence ushered in a period of mass hysteria in 1909. Numerous sightings of the Jersey Devil prompted businesses and schools to close for several days as it terrorized an area from Southern New Jersey into Philadelphia.

Bullets and even cannonballs have been entirely ineffective in hunting the Jersey Devil, which is part of the reason this lone creature has existed as long as it has. It has even survived electrocution when accidentally tangled in electrical wires. There is no known method for capturing and/or killing the Beast, though many Monster Hunters have tried.

Some insist that the Jersey Devil has never been a threat to anything other than livestock, but I have my doubts. Not all bodies found in Pine Barrens can be attributed to the mafia that uses the area as a dumping ground. I do believe that Monster Hunters should be on the Hunt for this wicked being. Just beware that not everyone considers the legend to be feared. The state of New Jersey has even adopted the Jersey Devil as their hockey team's mascot. I wouldn't be surprised to find a full blown tourist trade has evolved to turn the feared demon into a cute little collectible in an attempt to make a few bucks off the beast.

Gargoyle

Origin: Supernatural
Locale: Global
Indentifying traits: Stone in daytime
Best Time to Hunt: Never. These are peaceful creatures
Threat Level: None

A winged creature that protects humans from evil by night and turns to stone in the daylight.

Gargoyles are rockin' on sunshine

They're big. They're scary. And they certainly go bump in the night. But Gargoyles are one very large exception to the rule that everything described in those terms is evil. Gargoyles are not only the most benevolent of the "Monsters" that people fear, they are also the most misunderstood. This is incredibly unfair to these noble creatures that, under the proper circumstances, can be a Monster Hunter's greatest ally.[5]

First, we need to consider what the average person knows of Gargoyles. Conveniently, it's not much. Most people dismiss them as rainspouts or ornamentation for buildings. That is partially true. The overwhelming majority of Gargoyles we see on the street are little more than carved or molded concrete that have no special abilities whatsoever. But they are useful in helping to hide the truth about the magical beings that share their name.

The word "Gargoyle" comes from the French word for throat, gargouille. This is further derived from the Latin word gurgulio, which also refers to the

gurgling sound water makes. Manmade Gargoyles were initially built as a means of directing rain flow away from a building. The Gargoyle in architecture serves both decorative and functional purposes that have very little to do with the creatures that concern us.

What the two types of Gargoyle have in common is the belief that they are a means of warding off evil. True, this is a superstitious belief that has no basis in fact for the ornamental Gargoyles, but it is the very mission in life of the Mystical Gargoyles.

5.   Certainly, they are among our more powerful allies.

The Gargoyles that Monster Hunters are concerned with are not the creation of man. Truthfully, we don't know how they came into being, whether they were naturally born or the result of some kind of spell. These magical beings are stone statues during the day, sitting atop buildings all over the world, appearing as innocent as the architectural Gargoyles they resemble.[6] But at night, these Monsters come to life, protecting the building that they reside on as well as the city or town they have made their home.

Relatively few people know that these stone Gargoyles come to life, which is for their benefit as well as ours. The reason is simple: People fear the unusual. The only proof you need of this is the very legend of the Gargoyle that has been accepted truth throughout history. The story of La Gargouille has been twisted through each retelling. It explains the origin of the Gargoyles we put on buildings while ignoring the cruel manner this noble being was treated at the hands of man. You see, the Gargoyle in the story of La Gargouille is the villain.

The French legend concerns a dragon-like creature that supposedly terrorized the town of Rouen and surrounding areas in the seventh century. La Gargouille breathed fire, swallowed men whole and could devour a ship. This would put it on the top of the danger list for Monster Hunters if any of it were true. Certainly one can understand how the uneducated people of the time would be affected by the mere idea of this Monster.

Villagers lived in fear of La Gargouille until St. Romanis killed it through one of any number of heroic methods that would have been completely useless in real life.[7] The body of La Gargouille was brought back to Rouen where it was set aflame. When the head refused to burn, it was mounted on a church as a warning to other Monsters. This began the tradition of architectural Gargoyles manufactured to ward off evil.

As I wrote earlier, a Monster like that would be at the top of a Hunter's attack list if any part of the story was actually true. All my research on Gargoyles indicates that that kind of behavior is totally out of character. The Gargoyles I know only wish to help. None breathe fire, though it would certainly be handy if they did.

6.   Technically the name for them would be "Grotesque," as water does not flow through them, but let's not nitpick.
7.   One story claims he was only armed with a crucifix, which has absolutely no effect on Gargoyles whatsoever.

Gargoyles are solitary creatures. They live on their own, claiming an entire town as their protectorate. They are incredibly possessive of their home, seeing themselves as responsible for keeping the streets and their people safe from criminals and Monstrous threats. They are sometimes willing to work with humans that prove themselves trustworthy. Though Gargoyles are intelligent creatures, they have no formal language, but they do seem to understand humans. I have been able to communicate with them through a series of verbal and nonverbal prompts.

Most Gargoyles are larger and considerably bulkier than the average human. They have incredibly strong wings to support their weight, allowing them to glide on air currents. Their hide is hard and thick, yet pliable, at nighttime. Some unknown power in the direct rays of the sun affects their skin, turning it to stone at sunrise. They are instinctively aware of the moment before they will turn so they can get themselves to a safe place before their bodies harden. It is a fascinating sight to watch a Gargoyle go from living being to stone statue. One that I recommend witnessing if you ever have the chance.

In their stone state, Gargoyles are vulnerable to attack as they can be dismantled is the same manner as any regular stone statue. It is important that their true identities remain a secret as there is no telling what could happen to them during the daylight hours when they are totally defenseless.

Golem

Origin: Supernatural
Locale: Global
Indentifying traits: Appears as a living statue
Effective Weaponry: Spells
Ineffective Weaponry: Guns and knives.
Best Time to Hunt: Any
Worst Time to Hunt: None
Threat Level: Moderate

An artificial human composed of clay brought to life through magic and manipulated by its creator to do his bidding.

Even the best intentions can lead to evil.

According to legend, the first Golem was created in the sixteenth century by a rabbi in Prague to protect his people from the pogroms and anti-Semitic attacks focused on the Jewish ghettos of the city. Though the stories vary, it is commonly held that the rabbi molded the Golem out of clay from a riverbank, bringing it to life through a series of prayers and incantations. The rabbi then wrote the word shem ("name") on a piece of parchment and placed it in the Golem's mouth and etched the word emet ("truth") onto the statue's forehead.

Once alive, the Golem protected the community against attackers using its enhanced strength. But as the creature grew more powerful, the violence it wrought increased, eventually causing fear among the very people it was made to protect. The rabbi was forced to destroy it. He did this by removing the first letter "e" from emet, changing the word to met, which means "death."

The word, Golem, translates into "body without a soul" or to be more precise "cocoon." Though the creature comes from the Jewish tradition, Golems know no religion and can be controlled by anyone working the proper spell. These living statues are linked with their creator through a mystical state of consciousness and only remain animated as long as that bond is active. This makes the creator almost entirely responsible for their slave's actions. Even though a Golem possesses no intellect of its own they have been known override their instructions and lash out in senseless violence.

Golems are harder to control the stronger they become. Poorly constructed ones are never really under their master's powers. For that reasons, it is strongly suggested that no human should ever create one. Even when they are made with the best of intentions, these situations rarely end well for anyone, much less the creator. Of course, when these things go out of control—as they always do—that's when the Monster Hunter is called in to save the day.

When someone warns you not to do something, don't do it.

To repeat: No one should ever attempt to construct a Golem for any reason. However, it helps to examine the process of how they are made so we can know how to destroy them. The following primer will give you some of the basic steps that go into building a Golem. Please note that I am intentionally leaving out a few points to ensure that my words cannot be used to create evil.

Most people will tell you that it takes years of study and discipline in the mystical arts to create a Golem. Even then, the artificial being is difficult to control. Far too many novice practitioners think that they can command these automatons, which usually results in the most violent members of their breed. The best source of information on the "recipe" for creating a Golem is the Sefer Yetzira Book of Creation. But even this famous tome has inspired contradictory translations.

It is universally accepted that a Golem should be shaped into a figure resembling a human, but that is not written in stone.[8] The statue can take any form the creator chooses, but it will still only have traditional Golem powers. Just because someone gives it wings does not mean it will fly. A specific "magic word" is used to bring it to life. That word can be etched into the clay or written on parchment and fed to it. The best clay to use in the sculpting the Golem should be virgin soil that has never been touched by humankind, which is difficult to find these days.

Once the Golem is complete, the creator will have total control over its actions. Be warned that they are incredibly literal and accept their commands exactly as dictated. One should always take special care as a simple turn of phrase may result in a cataclysmic disaster. Even at its most uncontrollable, the Golem is incapable of killing its master. That is something the Monster Hunter may need to do on his own.

8.   Sorry. Couldn't resist.

A Golem is only as good as its maker.

Golems possess superior strength and are invulnerable to attack, but otherwise have no special magical abilities. Its body is composed of mystically hardened clay that deflects bullets. It is even impervious to most explosive devices. A Golem will never tire. It will continue to fight until it has conquered its opponent. You will never win a hand-to-hand confrontation with one. Conveniently, you never have to try.

A Golem shares a mystical state of consciousness with its master. Sever that connection and you will render the Golem inert. This is where your Hunting skills could use a bit of sleuthing. It is rare that the Golem's creator will announce his intentions. Most of these people aren't stupid. They know that the easiest way to defeat the Golem is by confronting its master. Since Golems can't speak, it's not like one is going to give you the answer on its own. I have had some success following Golems back to their masters, but this can be a risky endeavor. I prefer determining who benefits most from the pattern of attacks. Find the person with motive and you'll find the Golem's motivator.

Once you have the creator, it usually is just a case of having him recite a reversal spell or, as in the case of legend, alter the words etched into the Golem to disarm it. That could take some convincing, but then it's up to you to decide how much pressure needs to be applied. Don't forget that the Golem acts as an arm of its creator. The guilt of its actions lies solely in the human who commands it.

Not every master will be convinced to let his or her slave free. Killing the master would raise some interesting moral and (more importantly) legal questions. As Monster Hunters, we can't just go around killing humans. At the same time, it's difficult to try someone in a court of law when the only evidence is a creature that very few juries believe in. Once you have solved this moral quandary and found the proper means to render the Golem lifeless, you can easily destroy the body. And you should, since you don't need anyone else waking it up.

Werewolf

Origin: Supernatural
Locale: Global
Indentifying traits: A huge wolf
Effective Weaponry: Silver bullets
Ineffective Weaponry: Traditional bullets
Best Time to Hunt: Night of the full moon
Worst Time to Hunt: Night of the full moon
Threat Level: High

A cursed human that, through supernatural means, turns into a hulking, murderous wolf on the night of the full moon.

The Werewolf bite is far worse than its bark.

It was one of the original "Big Four" Horror Monsters[9] that struck fear in the hearts of moviegoers, filling their nightmares with images of the wild predator. The Werewolf of movies today is seen more as a pitiable creature, a cursed human totally out of control of its own body on the night of the full moon. The true Werewolf is somewhere in between: still terrifying in its ferocity, but also tragic in its sad tale.

The Werewolf is one of the most challenging Monsters that a Hunter will encounter. Not just because of its fierce predatory skills, but because of the moral implications we face when taking one on. No one chooses to become a Werewolf. At least, I've never encountered anyone who willingly made the decision. For all but a few nights of the year, the Werewolf is a regular human with all the strengths and weaknesses, the virtues and flaws that we possess. On the night of the full moon the cursed being experiences a complete loss of humanity in their altered state, no longer guided by a moral compass. It attacks on instinct, feeding off the flesh of whatever crosses its path.

I would like nothing more than to tell you that a Werewolf can be controlled. That it can be locked up on the night of the full moon and free to roam every other night of the year. To live a normal life. But that is simply not true. Werewolves refuse to be caged no matter how much their human side wants it. In its animal form the Werewolf will exploit any weakness in the cage until it escapes. If escape is truly impossible, it will eventually take its own life in a horrific act of self-mutilation. The only truly humane way of dealing with a Werewolf is to kill it. Not just to protect others, but to put it out of its own misery as well.

9.   Along with Vampires, Frankenstein's monster, and Mummies.

Werewolves are supernatural predators ... emphasis on "super."

Like so many of the other Monster tales we encounter, stories of men turning into wolf-like creatures date back to Ancient Greece. And these stories are almost always about men. Even the various words associated with this curse are derived from the word "man." Werewolf itself translates from the Old English "wer" for man. The alternate Latin root for the name, lycanthrope, is based on the Greek work lukanthropos, wherein "lukos" refers to the wolf and "anthropos" is man. In spite of the name game, the Werewolf curse affects both men and women indiscriminately and equally. A female Werewolf is no more difficult to combat than the male. And no less vicious.

The Werewolf curse is transferred through two methods. Primarily it is inherited when the genetic mutation is passed from parent to child. There is no absolute guarantee that the child of a cursed person will inherit the gene, however. Studies show that as long as one of the parents is fully human, there is a fifty-fifty chance that the child will be human as well. The gene will not exert itself until puberty. This allows the child to live a perfectly normal life up to the teen years while his or her parents usually spend that same period worrying what will become of their child. In cases where both parents carry the mutated gene, it is certain that the child will be a Werewolf as well.

The other means of transferring the curse is through infection of the bloodstream from a Werewolf bite. The gene for the Werewolf infection is carried through the saliva. Once the gene infects the human victim, there is no known cure. This method is incredibly rare since Werewolves hardly ever leave their victims alive.

It's a little known fact of our trade that most of the human victims that have been infected through Werewolf bites were formerly Monster Hunters since they are among the few people with the ability to survive a Werewolf attack. Not to be immodest, but the number of my apprentices who survived to turn rather than dying from the initial attack is a bit of a testament to my ability to properly train for combat against werewolves.[10]

One might think that all this talk of genetics and infection would mean that Werewolves are Monsters of natural or scientific creation. While they possess aspects of those origins, Werewolf traits are more supernatural in design, making them weighted more in the unnatural side of Unnatural Beasts. The most familiar of these traits is the trigger that turns them on the night of the full moon. Many have conjectured as to what qualities of the moon hold this kind of sway over the Werewolf curse, but science has yet to find an answer.

The change into a Werewolf is a particularly painful experience, requiring bones to be broken and reset and the very skin stretched to inhuman proportions. Every aspect of the wolf form is multiple times larger than the average wolf. The claws are sharper, the teeth more vicious. Strength, speed, and agility are increased. Although the wolf body does not possess any aspect of human consciousness, it does retain the intelligence, making it a fierce combatant. Every one of the Werewolf's senses is heightened as well. It can track scents across miles. Night vision is more acute. Hearing more accurate. The Werewolf also has supernatural regenerative abilities, able to heal from the deepest wounds in minutes.

Once the sun has risen, the wolf body reverts to its human form until the next full moon. Those cursed can take little solace in the fact that they have no memory of their time spent as a wolf. As you'd expect, most people don't want to recall the images of destruction they had wrought. But to many it is just as horrific to never know the full extent of the destruction they caused.

10.   I always felt badly about having to kill those same apprentices later when they turned.

Silver is the everything metal.

Tracking the Werewolf is surprisingly easy since it leaves a fair amount of death and destruction in its wake. Its oversized paws make prints that are easily distinguished from other animals, including the smaller wolf cousins. The big problem with tracking a Werewolf is that the closer you get to one, the more likely it is that it's also tracking you.

In all honesty, the easiest way to kill a Werewolf is to determine who it is in its human form and kill it before the full moon. As a human, it has the same strengths and weaknesses as any person. It is entirely vulnerable to traditional weapons. You just need to be sure to destroy the remains before the night of the full moon or you risk regeneration. The only problem is that you are then killing a human, which is harder for some Monster Hunters to face. Unlike the human that controls a Golem and forces it to do evil, the human form of the Werewolf bears no responsibility for its animalistic actions.

Combating the Werewolf in wolf form may be emotionally easier, but it is a thousand times more physically challenging with the added risk of infection if you're bitten. Still, we are Monster Hunters, not Human Hunters. If you're not willing to run that risk, stay out of the business.

I will tell you right now, you alone are no match against a Werewolf at full strength. Your best bet is to weaken the Werewolf at the start of any confrontation by poisoning it. This will not kill the creature, but it will make it a more manageable opponent. The herb wolfsbane is the most toxic poison to Werewolves.[11] Mix it with animal remains you use as bait and wait for the Werewolf to ingest it before the attack. Just be sure to remain upwind of the Werewolf because it will always chose live prey over dead meat. You should also carry the Wolfsbane on your body as it is an effective repellent that will disguise your scent. Arrowheads dipped in the herb are also useful for slowing the creature, but unless the tip is silver, even a shot to the heart will not be fatal.

The only way to kill a Werewolf is to deliver a fatal blow with a weapon made of silver. The precious metal inhibits the Werewolf's regenerative powers once it enters the bloodstream. However, the metallic toxin is not fatal on its own. The silver instrument must cut through the heart in order to provide a permanent solution.

11.   Other effective poisons include Mistletoe, Mountain Ash, and Rye.

Werebeasts

Werewolves are the most serious threat among the various species that experience therianthropy (i.e. the metamorphosis of humans into animals), but they are far from the only example of this phenomenon. Pardon the pun, but shape-shifters come in many forms and the humans that turn into animals are not limited to the family of wolves.

Werecat: Originating in the legends of India, this human can take the form of a member of the cat family. Although the type of cats range from the domestic cat to the larger predators including tigers and jaguars, the human can only hold one cat form. He does not switch between different cat bodies. As a result, these creatures come in varying threat levels from Low to Moderate.

Werehyena or Hyena Men: Found largely in Africa, the Hyena Man actually begins life as hyena and grows to assume the shape of a human instead of the other way around. Threat Level: Moderate.

Werefox: Japanese legend tells of a female fox that took human form and fell in love with a man whom she married and bore his children. When the husband found out her secret, he accepted her for what she was and she went on to split her time, spending her nights as a woman and days as a fox. Threat Level: Low.

Shark Man: The Hawaiian Shark Man is believed to be the son of a mortal woman and a shark god. He turns into a shark when he enters the water and is weakened the longer he stays away from the ocean.

Skin-Walker

Skin-Walkers are humans that can shape-shift into a variety of animal forms through witchcraft. They can be found globally, but the highest concentration is in the Southwestern United States where their stories are told extensively in Native American legend, though the tales vary from tribe to tribe. Among Native Americans, a Skin-Walker is considered the highest level of evil black magic practitioner. A human trains for years at the craft before taking part in the initiation ritual that requires the sacrifice of a member of their family to accept the power by breaking cultural taboo.

Once the initiation is complete, the Skin-Walker can shift into the form of any animal it chooses[12] once it covers itself in the skin of that animal. The transformation only happens at night. While it is in that form the Skin-Walker is faster and more agile than the average human. In some cases it can even fly. The sheer variety of animal bodies is takes on makes it difficult prey to track.

In the animal guise a Skin-Walker can mimic the sounds of that animal, but the transformation is not perfect. For some unknown reason, Skin-Walkers are generally unable to replicate the animal's stride, leaving the careful observer able to identify the Skin-Walker, oddly enough, by the way that it walks.

12.   Although they usually have one preferred form.

There are many myths associated with the Skin-Walker. The Navajo believe that the creature can be killed simply through an accusation, by saying the person's name followed by the phrase, "You are a Skin-Walker." Three days later the person is said to die. Another belief is that if you lock eyes with a Skin-Walker it can absorb itself into your body. I have yet to see this in practice, but I try to avoid direct eye contact rather than take the risk.

Guns and other traditional weapons are useless against a Skin-Walker in animal form. In fact, physical confrontation with a Skin-Walker in either its human or animal body is not recommended as the magic protects it from harm. The creature is sensitive to light and shies away from it, but I've yet to find a way to convert that into a weapon. Covering your body with corn pollen, cedar ash, or juniper berries will protect you from a Skin-Walker's supernatural powers, but they have no direct effect on the creature itself.

Your only chance for stopping a Skin-Walker is to determine the identity of its human form, track it back to its home and perform one of the rituals devised by shamans to strip it of its power. Once powerless, you can easily kill the human body. For those squeamish about killing a human, remember that the Skin-Walker is in control of its actions when it embodies an animal. However, if you prefer to turn the person over to the authorities, you certainly can. The Skin-Walker has, at the very least, killed a family member or else it would never have become an Unnatural Beast.

Wendigo

Wendigo is one of dozens of names for a Native American evil being indigenous to Canada. It is a cannibalistic killer that preys on anyone unfortunate enough to enter the woods that it inhabits. Reports vary on the look of the creature, but most agree that the Wendigo is a fifteen foot tall, thin, monstrous beast with sallow skin, a mouth full of sharp, yellow fangs and long claws that can slice open its victims. The creature's sole motivation is to devour human flesh. It spends its entire existence fulfilling that need.

The Wendigo's hunting technique combines human intelligence with animal instincts. It first plays a cruel game of cat and mouse, emitting whispering noises and other eerie sounds that eventually cause its prey to flee in terror and straight into its trap. Death comes quickly at that point as the Wendigo enters a state of feeding frenzy. There are numerous reports of the beast making a single meal out of an entire hunting party. Oddly, the Wendigo is only interested in human flesh, leaving the other forest residents alone. Its singular focus on human flesh is paired with an insatiable hunger. It is always on the hunt for more food.

According to legend, a human can become a Wendigo when he or she practices cannibalism, but I have yet to find proof of that story. The Wendigo can possess humans, both those who come to the creature willingly as well as innocent victims. Over time, the possession will turn the victim into a cannibal. Eventually the person's body will change into a creature that resembles the Wendigo, though it will be smaller and less powerful. Unlike the Werewolf or Skin-Walker, this change is permanent and irreversible. Only a shaman can exorcise the Wendigo spirit during the early stages of the possession.

The Wendigo does share many traits with the Werewolf, which often confuses people into thinking that they are one and the same. The Wendigo also has advanced strength, speed, and agility along with the increased regenerative abilities. It is said that the wind and cold announce the creature's approach as it can affect the temperature. Conversely, it fears fire, but that alone will not keep the creature away.

Silver weapons are the best method for attacking the Wendigo, although iron and steel are also effective. Either blades or bullets will weaken the creature if you can get close enough to inflict serious injury. But the only way to kill it is by a silver blade to the chest. This will shatter its frozen heart. Once killed, your work is still not done. Using your silver blade you must dismember the body, salting and burning each piece and scattering its ashes. The heart must also be buried in a silver box in consecrated ground to ensure that the evil will not return.

Magic and mystery make up our history.

Unnatural Beasts exist in all corners of the world. They have grown along with the legends of indigenous peoples of every continent and evolved with humankind as we spread their stories across the Earth. Many of them are the worst combination of nature and magic, making them difficult to combat, but not impossible to kill. Being grounded in reality doesn't make them any less scary, although it somehow makes them seem more manageable.

And yet, the mingling of magic and nature can sometimes result in a creature of noble breeding and heroic virtue, like the Gargoyle. Or one of surprising humanity and love, like the Werefox. Magic is neither good nor evil. It is often we humans that twist it into something else and are punished for our grandiose schemes.

Magic is also the cornerstone for many of the stories we learn as children about the creatures we could never imagine actually existing on Earth. This takes us from the unnatural to the fantastic. Creatures once believed to be of myth and legend in actual flesh and blood. There is magic ahead. And dragons. And unicorns. As we explore the Fantasy Creatures…

FANTASY CREATURES

Sometimes a fantasy can be the real thing.

Fantasy.

To the average person, that word conjures up genteel images of rainbows and unicorns, the stuff that sweet dreams are made of. These are the kinds of stories our parents tell us as children in the hopes of lulling us to sleep in a way that holds back the nightmares. But fans of the fantasy genre in literature and film know that creatures of darkness are also associated with the word. It's the big and scary Monsters that make our heroes all the more heroic for taking them on. It is also true that sometimes these cruel creatures do come wrapped in pretty packages.

Every being that a Monster Hunter encounters has a bit of the fantastical about it. Whether it is actual magic or the legend of magic based on ancient superstitions is something I've explored in my encounters with them and dissected in this tome. We've already discussed several Monsters that have a touch of magic about them. The Fantasy Creatures we now examine are almost all pure magic with impure intentions. But how does a mere mortal take on a fire-breathing Dragon? Many times that answer relies on a combination of magic and mortal weaponry. Not every solution for dealing with Monsters can be found at the end of a sword or the chamber of a gun. Sometimes the sound of a bell is enough to keep you safe, or a circle on the ground made of salt. Fantasy Creatures don't rely on traditional means for attack, so you need to be prepared for the untraditional defense if you want to survive.

Wanted: Undead or Alive

Can you kill a Unicorn? A cute, harmless little Unicorn that stands for all that is pure and virtuous in the world and has magical healing properties in its horn?

Should you kill a Unicorn? A vicious Unicorn that keeps to the shadows of the forest and can run a human through with its horn killing you in seconds and devouring your remains?

The greatest challenge to the Monster Hunter is not battling the creatures that we Hunt, it is the decision we face when we first come up against them. Which Monsters do we kill? Which do we capture? Which do we leave alone? What is the truth behind the legends?

Not everything that goes bump in the night is coming after you. Not every childhood fantasy is a dream come true. The moral implications of the Monster Hunter's work can keep anyone up at night. Sure, there are Hunters that kill indiscriminately, but that doesn't make them good at their job. The ones that can't decide, that are locked frozen with indecision are certainly bad at theirs. And usually dead. The properly trained Monster Hunter is able to make a split second decision on the nature of an opponent, fully aware that there is a fine line between being a hero and being a murderer.

How does a Monster Hunter make that call? Well, it is my hope that this collection of Hunter tips you've been reading can serve as a proper starting point for making such a decision. I have spent hours painstakingly committing my experiences to the pages of this tome to give you many of the facts you will need to know. I wish there was a way to create a list of creatures that you should immediately kill on sight, but that's difficult, if not impossible, to do. Every Monster is unique and every situation has its own set of rules. Let's just take a look at the most popular Monsters and see how your endgame must differ for each.

Zombies should be destroyed immediately, without hesitation. Their sole purpose in life is to eat human flesh, which can create more Zombies in the process. They do not have individual personalities. They are not useful sources of information. They are mindless machines. Decapitating them is no different that taking off the heads of one of those old Animatronic attractions at Disney World. Not to mention that they're already dead.

Vampires are different. They are equal in their killing machine status, but they have distinct personalities. I know I made a point earlier about how Hollywood's romanticizing of Vampires with a soul is a dangerous lie, but that wasn't entirely true. Who can say if there really aren't good Vampires out there? I certainly haven't seen any or heard of any encounters with one, but it's worth taking the time to understand what motivates the Vampire you are about to take on, if only to prepare you for battle. Even so, it is highly unlikely that you're going to accidentally stumble upon a good Vampire in your travels. A moment's hesitation can result in your death. But if you do question your actions, just remember that every Vampire has killed at least once.

Mummies, like Zombies, are already dead. So killing them takes on a different meaning. Rarely will you be destroying a soul. Usually you can take solace in the knowledge that you are actually helping it move on or return it to its resting place.

And finally, Werewolves. These are the hardest Monsters to take on, in my opinion. When they are not in their Werewolf guise, they are merely humans with little to no responsibility for their counterpart's actions. Killing a Werewolf is the most unpleasant moral challenge you will face. I know of a few Monster Hunters that retired after causing the death of one, unable to pick up a gun or knife again.

To kill or to capture is a tough decision. It's one of the most difficult choices you will face. The properly trained Monster Hunter is not just physically or mentally prepared, he or she needs to be emotionally strong as well.

Demon

Origin: Natural or Supernatural
Locale: Global and otherworldly
Identifying traits: Varied
Effective Weaponry: Holy Water,
Spells
Ineffective Weaponry: Traditional
Weapons
Best Time to Hunt: Night
Worst Time to Hunt: Day
Threat Level: High

Any of the race of creatures of supernatural origin that are typically seen as the
personification of evil.

There is more to Demon life than Heaven and Hell.

Demons are one of the greatest mysteries of the universe. No one knows for sure where they came from, no one knows what they ultimately want, and only a few people really understand how to deal with them.

World religions have attached vastly different definitions to the word "Demon" throughout the centuries. Some believe that a Demon is a benevolent creature that grants your wishes like the Genie in the lamp. One of the more popular modern beliefs is that a Demon is a fallen angel along the lines of Lucifer. I admit that I don't have all the answers.[1] A debate over whether Heaven and Hell exist is not something I intend to get into within these pages. The kinds of Hell on Earth I've witnessed lead me to believe that it's a moot point. Whether demons come from "Hell," "The Underworld" or some other Demon dimension is up for scholars to examine. I'm only worried about what to do with one when it gets here.

"Demon" has become a bit of a catchall word we've used to describe all manner of supernatural creature that we don't have an explanation for. Whether or not these are true demons is up to personal belief. For our purposes we will consider a Demon to be a malevolent supernatural creature of unknown origin. The way we deal with one varies depending on the individual Demon, but there are certain universal traits most Demons share that will assist us in dissecting their methods.

1.   But I have most of them.

No two Demons are alike ... and neither are their powers.

Demons as a race are the oldest Monsters you will face. Many of them have been around since before the dawn of time. They come in different strengths with the weaker Demons easy to dispatch by the thrust of a silver dagger while the strongest Demons are virtually impossible to take on. Luckily, Demons are aggressive and anti-social by nature. Their inability to cooperate is humanity's best defense.[2] If Demons ever got organized and worked together against us, the planet would be doomed.

Demonic powers are as varied as the Demons themselves. Some Demons have the ability to call on many supernatural weapons, while others can barely scratch up enough magic to enact a spell. It is important to identify the level of Demon you are dealing with before engaging in battle. The last thing you need is a fireball coming at you when you think all your enemy can do is levitate. The most prominent Demonic powers are the following:

Teleportation

Mind control

Possession

Energy bolts

Fireballs

Levitation

Telekinesis

2.   I've found that pitting two Demons against one another is the best way to take them on without putting yourself in direct harm.

Battling a demon can be Hell.

Like Mummies, the only way to deal with a demon is to determine its motivation. As I've said before, each Demon is different. The Demon's motivation is often what leads to its downfall. When you receive a call about a Demon the first thing you must do is research. Learn about the area the Demon is infesting and the history of its people. Demons tend to be attracted to a particular location with a specific objective in mind.

Demon Hunting requires the most amount of research of any Monster you will encounter. Thankfully, the advent of the internet has made this an easier task, but let's be honest, half the information online is useless rumors anyway. I highly recommend having a few historians and religious scholars on speed dial. Even if it turns out that Demons are not tied to any specific mythology, most world religions have been recording their existence for centuries and have the best archival information. There is enough information on Demons to fill libraries, but these are the basics you'll need to know for Demon Hunting:

- Physical combat with a Demon is not recommended. Even the weakest Demon is stronger than the average Monster Hunter.

- Magical weaponry is required. There is a vast black market trading in magical axes and enchanted swords. Stock up.

- An elemental understanding of magic is useful. Spells can be powerful weapons.

- Potion-making skills are beneficial as well.

- Demonic possession is another concern. Having a trained exorcist on call is recommended.

Dragon

Origin: Supernatural
Locale: Global
Indentifying traits: Size and scaly appearance
Effective Weaponry: Sword
Ineffective Weaponry: Explosives
Best Time to Hunt: Day
Worst Time to Hunt: Night
Threat Level: High

A huge, flying lizard-like creature that breathes fires, hoards treasures, and has a penchant for princesses or other maidens.

Dragons are a true tale as old as time.

It is one of the first Monsters we learn about as children. Stories of heroic knights rescuing young maidens from the clutches of a Dragon have woken the initial stirrings of interest in this field in more than one Monster Hunter. You can imagine the disappointment when the apprentice Hunter learns how unlikely it is that he or she will ever come across one.

Dragons are incredibly rare creatures. I've only encountered one in my entire career, although I did manage to fight it on two separate occasions. The first time left me on death's door with serious burns and a week-long hospital stay. The second time resulted in a new trophy for my library. Both of these experiences were with the same Dragon of the Western variety.

But first, a brief word about the Eastern Dragon.[3]

The Eastern Dragon is a long, scaled serpentine creature found predominantly in Asian countries. Though it has no wings, it can fly through supernatural means. It is considered a symbol of power, strength, and good luck and a sighting of the creature is an auspicious event. The Eastern Dragon can control the rains and is credited with bringing much needed water to drought-stricken regions. It is a noble creature that should not be hunted under any circumstance.

---

3.   The Eastern Dragon is sometimes referred to as the Chinese Dragon, however it can be found in most Asian lands.

The Western Dragon is a wicked creature.

The Monster Hunter's main foe of the Dragon family can be found in Europe and North America[4], which is why it is commonly referred to as the "Western Dragon." It is the traditional Maiden-kidnapping evil star of fairy tales, with a winged, green scaly body, a long tail, talons on its four feet, and a reptilian head that breathes fire. It can grow to be over fifty feet in length.

The Dragon is a long-lived creature. Though there are not many in existence, it is believed that each Dragon has survived in seclusion for hundreds of years. The Dragon is highly intelligent, though it does not speak human language as some stories would have you believe.

As a solitary being, a Dragon makes its lair in remote locations as varied as swamps and deserts, though the preference is for forest and mountain caves. With population expansion, however, this is becoming increasingly difficult. The Dragon is a natural hoarder, which is why many a treasure hunter seek it out. But be warned that Dragon treasure is usually cursed and can only bring harm to anyone that touches it. The true treasure in a Dragon can be found in its body.

A Dragon is somewhere between Cryptid and true Fantasy creature. Its magical properties make it a high-value target because a Dragon's body can be used in any manner of way.

- The nearly impregnable scaly hide makes effective bulletproof armor.

- Dragon's blood has magical properties, but in its pure form it can be poisonous.

- Distilled through any number of processes, however, Dragon's blood can slow aging or heal any number of maladies.

- Properly captured Dragon flame can provide an eternal source of light or warmth, impossible to douse through human means.

- A taste of Dragon saliva will allow humans to communicate with the animals.

- Dragon tears have been known to clear up acne.

4.   If you look hard enough.

Dragons are made of tougher stuff.

Dragon Hunting is a particularly challenging skill to master as the modern Dragon does all that it can to avoid human contact. That's not to say that this creature never has an encounter with humans. It has a particular taste for our flesh that needs to be sated from time to time. In the past, a Dragon would terrorize towns for its food, but today it is stealthier, preferring to pick off meals and return to its secret lair unnoticed. An impressive feat for a huge flying creature.

In the past, a Dragon would be done in by its hubris, thinking it was invulnerable until some noble knight came along to prove it wrong with a sword to the chest. This didn't happen as often as the stories would lead us to believe, but enough to teach all Dragons a valuable lesson about protection. Today, finding a Dragon is almost as difficult as fighting one.

The Dragon is a skilled marksman, able to precisely aim its Dragon flame to only take out an intended target and avoid further damage. Following random scorch marks isn't always an indication of Dragon activity. Its tail is effective at sweeping away footprints when it isn't traveling by air. In flight, it keeps just above the tree line to avoid detection. Your best bet is to track reports of missing herds of cattle or sheep. The odds are that some kind of Monster is behind this. In these days of ecotourism, we also hear more about groups of missing humans. This limits the search as not all Monsters can take on groups of humans as well as a Dragon.

The Dragon's most effective weapon is its fire breath. I suggest heat protective clothing as a must. Avoid anything made of Dragon scales as it taunts your opponent unnecessarily. You also need to watch for both ends of the dragon as the tail can inflict as much destruction as the fire breath. Some Dragons have barbed tails with a fast acting poison.[5]

It is almost impossible to inflict damage to the Dragon hide, but every Dragon has a single chink in its armor. The only known way to destroy a Dragon is to find that weak spot; someplace where the scales are unprotected. It may not always be the supposedly soft underbelly, which is actually kind of hard. Study your opponent when you engage in battle. The Dragon knows its weakness. It will protect it instinctively.

Once you determine the soft spot, running it through with a sword or a masterfully aimed gunshot is all you need to do. It doesn't have to be the heart or the brain. Even the most inconsequential placement will cause the Dragon to bleed out as the skin cannot heal around the wound. Once the cut is inflicted, run because death is not always immediate.

5.   Trust me, I've witnessed this first hand.

Giant

Origin: Natural (Mostly)
Locale: Global
Indentifying traits: Enormous Size
Effective Weaponry: Heavy weapons
Ineffective Weaponry: Smaller weapons
Best Time to Hunt: Day
Worst Time to Hunt: Night
Threat Level: Moderate

Generic term for any oversized humanoid creature with cannibalistic tendencies.

Sometimes the bigger they are the easier it is to make them fall.

A Giant (or Giantess) can come in all shapes and sizes. There is no one uniform explanation for them or shared history. Every country has Giants that range from simply oversized humans to magical beings of immense proportions.

Giant humanoid Monsters have been the protagonists in heroic tales throughout history. The word "Giant" is derived from the *Gigantes* offspring of Gaea and has been used to describe other Greek monsters like the Cyclopes as well as the Frost and Rock Giants of Norse mythology. Human Giants are the least feared of Giants, but they can still cause a fair amount of trouble.

A Human Giant served the inspiration for the tale of Jack and the Beanstalk, though I can assure you it did not live in a castle in the clouds. A Giant will traditionally hide away with a modest number of its brethren in secluded valleys exiling itself from average-sized people. The traditional Giant is an oversized human that shares many of our strengths and weaknesses, just multiplied by its size. In spite of its incredible strength, it does tend to be slow-witted and can be easily fooled.

Tracking a Giant is a relatively simple task as the ground tends to shake when it walks. Be warned that the creature does have a flair for throwing boulders when confronted, but as long as you think creatively, you should be able to best one.

Obviously, a Giant should never be engaged in hand-to-hand combat, but most traditional heavy weapons will be effective. Though its senses are heightened like everything else about it, the Giant cannot smell the blood of Englishman or anyone else. In addition to heavy weapons, I suggest looking to the children's story for inspiration and use the own Giant's size against it. They are many ways you can use its size and weight to trick a Giant into capturing itself if you are clever enough. Once a Giant is down, it is surprisingly difficult for it to get itself back up. Capture and rehabilitation are recommended in this case as the human Giant is traditionally misunderstood and does not intend to inflict most damage it causes.

Troll

Trolls are also larger than average humanoid creatures, though they are not as big as your average Giant. They are often confused with Ogres in stories, but the two are distant relatives that have little in common.

The typical Troll is a skilled metal worker, forging first-rate weaponry. In the past, Trolls sold these weapons to humans as they are not natural fighters themselves.[6] That's not to say that Trolls are peaceful creatures. They have a history of kidnapping women and children, carrying them off never to be seen again.

Trolls are also a greedy race, known for stealing property when homes are left unattended. Unfortunately, due to their size, they often destroy the home in the process of their theft. The children's story about a Troll living under bridges and charging a fee to anyone that will pass is based on a true story, though it was a lone example of a Troll that lived outdoors, for reasons I will explain in a moment.

The Troll is an ugly, hairy beast. It often sports a hunched back due to the confines of the underground hovels it resides that tend to be too small for its body. It can also be found in mountain caves or any deep, dark recesses of the Earth. Similar to Gargoyles, a Troll will turn to stone under the rays of the sun. This transformation, however, is permanent, which is why I suggest always battling a Troll during the daytime. If the Troll can be lured out of its home, the sunlight will take care of the problem. As Trolls tend to be active at night, it is best to track them during this time, but not engage them until near dawn.

Trolls hate noise and can be driven away by any loud din. In particular, the sound of church bells is quite disturbing to a Troll, but it needs to be a live sound. Recorded noises have little to no effect, no matter how loud the volume is turned. Placing mistletoe around the house is a common Troll repellent that serves as good protection from their thieving ways if you ever go on vacation. It also provides a good distraction to keep the Troll off guard and force it out into the sunlight during combat.

6.   Considering that the market for hand-forged weaponry is not as lucrative as it was in the past, it is possible that they have lost some of this talent over time.

Ogre

Ogres, as mentioned earlier, are related to Trolls, but they are not as violent or thieving. They are more similar in appearance to human Giants than Trolls, and are not actually green as Hollywood would have us believe. Random Trolls have been known to enjoy the taste of human flesh, but that is more of a rare treat for them and not their basic diet.

The fascinating thing about the Ogre is the vast difference in appearance between the male and female. The Male Ogre is among the ugliest of humanoid creatures you will encounter. It has an overly large head, wild, unruly hair, a huge protruding belly, and a strong body odor that will allow you to track it with ease. This brute is rather oafish and can be fooled with even the most basic trap.

The female Ogre is almost an exact opposite in description. She is quite fetching, in spite of her disproportionate size. Most are cunning beyond that of the average human and a challenge to even a skilled Monster Hunter. Many of my contemporaries have been lured into an Ogre trap after falling for the wiles of a female of the species.

A steel blade is your best weapon against an Ogre as they are naturally repulsed by this metal. The key thing to remember is that there are good and evil Ogres just like there are similar types of people. Though they do have a taste for human flesh, most have found ways to suppress that craving in exchange for living a life of solitude where it just wants to be left alone.[7] The Ogre is a perfect example of the type of Monster a Hunter should get to know before an attack. Oftentimes, simply capturing Ogres and relocating them to areas away from an easily frightened human population is enough to ensure the safety of all beings involved. It isn't always fair to force an Ogre to move from its home, but history has proven that Ogres and humans cannot coexist in harmony.

7.   This is something that movie got right.

Gremlin

The Gremlin is a relatively new entry in the Monster Hunter bestiary, coming into prominence during World War II. Airmen of Britain's Royal Air Force are credited with the initial reports of this pest, though further research has shown evidence of its existence dating back to the dawn of the Industrial Age. The name taken from the Old English gremian, meaning "to vex," which is a fitting description for the little Monster.

The average Gremlin is only about eighteen inches tall. Reports vary on a proper description of the creature, but most agree that it has a hairless body, oversized eyes, and large ears that are often depicted like plane wings in cartoons.[8] Some Gremlin sightings have also reported it to wear human-style clothing trimmed to its smaller size. The marine Gremlin is said to have webbed feet and fins, but I have not documented any evidence of this as the amphibian breed is incredibly rare.

8.   Once again, I must caution you not to envision Hollywood's image of Gremlins as you will find yourself in a lot of trouble if you wait for the sun to take care of them for you.

The Gremlin is a mischievous devil, obsessed with interfering with technology and mechanics with a particular desire to sabotage aircraft. It was found in abundance during World War II on both the Axis and Allies sides and credited with the mid-air destruction of planes that simply fell apart during flight. Though some of that was surely the result of faulty workmanship or the effects of war on a plane, there was more than enough documented cases of airmen witnessing these little devils in the cabin or on the wings to support the belief in them at the time.

The Gremlin primarily makes its home in underground burrows, oftentimes beneath the tarmac of airfields where it can slip into planes and cause turmoil during flight. As technology has expanded into our everyday lives, the Gremlin has multiplied in number and in interests. It is now often the cause of faulty devices used in the home, experiencing a boom in the population explosion around the time VCRs became commonplace in the average residence.

Some people believe that the Gremlin is related to some of the more mischievous races of Fairy, but I have found no link. In fact, the creature does not seem to possess any magic at all. It really is more like a pest than a real threat to the average Monster Hunter. Still, the pranks it plays have been responsible for air crashes that resulted in loss of life. I believe that Gremlins make good training Monsters for apprentices as they rarely pose much of a problem for a novice Hunter. The suggested method of Hunt would be to capture the Gremlins and relocate them to a Gremlin containment facility. These small prisons are relatively new and specialize in keeping Gremlins occupied by providing them with a steady stream of smaller mechanics to play with.

Unicorn

Origin: Supernatural
Locale: Global
Indentifying traits: Spiral horn on forehead
Effective Weaponry: Not applicable
Ineffective Weaponry: Not applicable
Best Time to Hunt: Night of the full moon
Worst Time to Hunt: Night of the new moon
Threat Level: None (Unless challenged)

One of the most popular fantasy creatures, the Unicorn is one of the purest beings on the planet, though that does not mean it can't handle itself in a fight.

A Unicorn sighting is a once in a lifetime experience.

The mention of a Unicorn automatically brings up an image of rainbows and white fluffy clouds for most people. Of all the creatures a Monster Hunter encounters, the Unicorn is by far the one with the best press. But the first question one must face when facing one down is whether or not that reputation is earned.

Like several of the other fantasy creatures explored in this issue, the Unicorn is one of the oldest beings on the planet. There are stories of Unicorns in the earliest tales of man. Though the description may change, the single-horned quadruped is universal in legend, but also incredibly rare in actual life experience.

To be honest, I believed the Unicorn to be a myth for most of my life. I had a difficult time comprehending how a creature that was supposedly the epitome of all that is good and pure could exist on this planet considering many of the horrors I have witnessed. It wasn't until one of my two particularly vicious Dragon battles in the forests of Romania that I saw the light.

This was the first of my encounters with said Dragon. It was also the less successful. The Dragon's barbed tale pierced my body, cutting a deep gash into my chest. Luckily for me, the Dragon flew off without finishing the job, but I was as good as dead. I could feel the poison working its way into my body. As I struggled to remain conscious and drag myself back to the radio in my vehicle, all my strength left me. I managed to roll onto my back to get one last glimpse of sunlight before it all went dark.

At first I thought I was seeing a vision, but it was real. A glowing white steed stepped out from between the trees with a flowing mane, imperial manner, and a single spiral horn in the center of its forehead. It was a Unicorn. I don't know why it exposed itself to me as I had lost my purity many years before, but that Unicorn tipped its horn into my wound and I could feel the poison receding. The wound healed itself. By the time I'd regained my strength, the Unicorn was gone. All that was left was my newfound belief.[9]

9.   And a few second-degree burns from the Dragon.

Unicorns are truly unique.

Rarer than rare, many scholars believe that the Unicorn is a genuinely unique creature; that there is only one in existence that has the power to teleport around the world through magical means. I don't know if the Unicorn I encountered was the lone Unicorn on Earth or one of an extreme few, but I count myself lucky to have seen it.[10]

Descriptions of the Unicorn have evolved throughout history. It has changed in size from the hulking body of an elephant[11] to the more popular form of a goat before ultimately settling on its current body similar to a horse. Whether these descriptions came from people that simply misidentified other animals or the Unicorn truly evolved over time remains one of the many mysteries surrounding the magical creature. All I can say for sure is that the current guise of the Unicorn matches that of a small horse. It is white from head to bushy tail. The horn, or *Alicorn*, is parchment color. The hooves match those of a horse. They are not cloven like a goat as has been reported.

The Unicorn is one of the gentlest creatures a person may encounter. It is also impossible to tame and fierce in battle when challenged. Its spiral horn can pierce any substance. A human attacker has little chance against it. Fortunately, very few people actually believe the Unicorn is real. Those that do Hunt the Unicorn as a trophy or to shave off some of the mystical healing properties of its horn are rare. Their Hunts usually end in failure.

10.   And not just because it saved my life. Though that was an added bonus.
11.   Some believe this creature was simply confused with a rhinoceros.

I'd be reluctant to include tips for Hunting the Unicorn if I feared for its safety, but I have no doubt this noble creature (or creatures) can sufficiently protect itself. I do believe that the benefits of human-Unicorn contact far outweigh the negatives and I trust that those schooled in my belief system when it comes to good and evil will share in my opinion of the Unicorn.

No matter the mythology, the Unicorn is often seen as a spiritual guide. It is said to have magical powers over nature and the ability to tame other animals in its presence.[12] The Unicorn has also been a portent of notable change and sightings have preceded great upheaval in the world. According to rumor, as long as humans continue to behave in hatred and greed, the Unicorn will remain hidden in the wild.

The Unicorn is drawn to water. Its spiritual powers are linked to the phases of the moon, which is why it is most often sighted on the night of the full moon. As the traditional belief goes, it is a creature of purity and can only be tamed by a virgin. Throughout history this has translated into a virginal maiden, but I believe that gender is unimportant. Traditionally, the virgin would sit in an open field until the Unicorn approached and laid its head in her lap. At that point hunters would ensnare it and take it back to their king. Mind you, I have never found any records proving that this method was anything more than an apocryphal.

As my experience proves, those who are (ahem) somewhat less pure can lay eyes on the creature. My only explanation is that the Unicorn may be naturally drawn to those in need, appearing from nowhere to render aid in extreme situations. It is for that reason, I believe that humans and Unicorn(s) should find a way to connect and live together in unison. I only fear that our society isn't quite there yet.

12.   In spite of this, it is believed that lions are their natural enemy.

Mermaid

Mermaids may get the notoriety, but Merfolk come in both genders and are equally dangerous. Merfolk are amphibious beings, able to breathe in fresh air or underwater through razor-thin gills in their necks that are nearly invisible to the naked eye. As most of you already know, they have the tail of a fish, but the head and torso of a human. They can, in fact, transform themselves into full humans for brief periods of time, but they can never travel too far from their ocean home or they will die.

Mermen are just as plentiful as their female counterparts, but it is the Mermaid that has become more of a fixture in marine legend both as a playful distraction for a lone sailor or, more fittingly, as a portent for doom. Don't let the beautiful image of the maiden fool you. A Mermaid sighting can easily end in death.

The Mermaid is a particularly vain being, almost always carrying a mirror or some reflective surface in which she can see herself. Her other most often seen accessory is a comb for brushing her long luxurious hair. Of course, living in the sea can be rough on a woman's hair, so I guess I can understand why they always seem to be combing it.

The Mermaid is famous for her beautiful voice and the stirring songs that she creates. Like the Greek Siren, these songs can be deadly, intentionally luring men to their deaths beneath the waves. This is not true of all Mermaids, however. It is believed that some of these songstresses do not have the intent to kill. They just simply forget that humans cannot breathe underwater and accidentally drown the men under the music's spell when the Mermaid refuses to let them go. In that case, you must be diligent in your Hunt to determine if your prey is worthy of battling, capture, or allowed to live her life.

Be warned that a Mermaid will offer to grant your wishes if captured, but this comes with strings attached. The Mermaid will almost always use trickery in granting that wish to ensure that she can gain her freedom and punish her captor in the process.

Mermen are a somewhat different opponent. The males of the species are almost always violent beings bent on destruction. Less attractive than their female counterparts in both appearance and attitude, the Merman can raise storms and wreck ships. A Merman rarely attacks on an individual basis, preferring to destroy an entire sailing vessel or cause massive damage to a coastline village. Though they have supernatural strength, they are no match for modern weaponry and a gun or even a harpoon is an effective deterrent.

Fairy

Origin: Supernatural
Locale: The Faerie Realm
Indentifying traits: Pointed ears
Effective Weaponry: Iron
Ineffective Weaponry: Traditional weapons
Best Time to Hunt: Never
Worst Time to Hunt: Always
Threat Level: High

A race of magical beings that exists in a realm just outside our own.

Fairies are the single most dangerous threat known to man.

That headline might make you laugh. Certainly the idea of fairies being a genuine threat would seem ludicrous to some. Even among my Monster Hunter brethren there are those who think I'm cracked when I say this. A fairy more dangerous than a Vampire? Than the Kraken? Absurd!

But true.

First, allow me to relieve you of the pleasant images of fairies in you might have in your mind. If you're thinking of the tiny little giggly beings with delicate wings that sprinkle pixie dust in their wake you can just file that image away. That description does fit some members of the Fairy race, but they are only one minor element. While most Fairies can shapeshift and magically alter their size, they generally take on human stature, but their beauty is unmatched on Earth or in the other realm they call home.

Fairies are a race of beings that are somewhere between human and spirit. They live in the Faerie Realm ruled by the two Faerie Courts. The Seelie Court is composed of Light Fairies or Summer Fey. The Unseelie Court belongs to the Dark Fey or Winter Fairies. Don't let them names fool you as both Courts are made up of Fairies that are peaceable along with others that can be unspeakably cruel. They are all charged with protecting the natural world and punishing humans who do not respect it.

The Realm of Faerie exists on a different plane. There is no geographical location for it on Earth. It is everywhere and nowhere at the same time. Always one step outside of human consciousness. Even so, some Fairies do choose to set up their invisible homes in the Earthly plane. This causes problems for any human unlucky enough to attempt building on that site.

Causing trouble is what Fairies do best. Be it minor pranks or deadly games, Fairies can tap into magic more powerful than any being on Earth. They can control and command the elements, turn nature against us, and drive humans to suicide with a mere thought. Why they don't simply take over and enslave humanity outright is a question I'm afraid to ask. Foolish people worry about the unlikely event of a Zombie infestation. My biggest fear is a Fairy invasion.

Be wary of any gift from a Fairy.

The Realm of Faerie is filled with vast treasures, both magical and earthly riches of gold and gemstones. To the best of my knowledge, no adult human has ever visited the Realm as it would be deadly to enter. Anyone that ventures into Fairy territory would be immediately taken to one of the two Courts and a death sentence for trespassing is almost guaranteed. Time moves differently in their Realm, but in inconsistent ways. Sometimes an hour in the Realm can equal a year on Earth or a minute on Earth is equal to a day in the Realm. There seems to be no rhyme or reason to this other than the whims of the Fair Folk.

Fairy codes are quite complex and the laws and treaties between the two Fairy Courts are practically impossible for most humans to understand. Offense is easily taken among their people and words must be chosen carefully. It almost doesn't matter for our purposes, however, since their rules of law do not relate to humans. They do what they want with mortals.

Although we cannot venture to their realm, Fairies easily walk among us on Earth. We simply can't see them for what they are. Fairies remain invisible unless they wish to be seen or they hide behind a magical glamour, camouflaging themselves in human guise.

Fairies are immortal, but they cannot reproduce, which means their numbers are constantly dwindling when they die by unnatural means. To combat this, they kidnap newborn human children and bring them into the Faerie Realm where they can be raised in magic and turned to Fairy Folk. The kidnapping Fairies will always leave a changeling in the place of the child so that the parents do not realize what has occurred. This changeling can either be a Fairy being that will be raised on Earth or it can be an inanimate object that will soon "die" leaving the human parents mourning for a child that lives on in the Faerie Realm.

Fairies enjoy nothing more than playing pranks on humans, but their definition of a prank is very different from ours. Being immortal, Fairies have little concept of time and what would be an afternoon's diversion for a human can be stretch on into years of torture in Fairy hands.

Fairy Rings are circles made by dancing fairies in the forests or other natural locations. If a human ever steps into a fairy ring he will get caught up in the dancing that could go endlessly for years. The problem is that Fairy music is so entrancing that once it is heard by human ears, it is nearly impossible to resist. Once trapped in a Fairy Ring, the only way out is for another human to pull you out, so long as that person does not step all the way into the ring as well.

Fairies have been known to make a human victim fall asleep for years or lose portions of time and memory. Eating and drinking fairy food will enslave humans as they will become entirely dependent on it, unable to find sustenance in human foods ever again. Fairies can also bestow gifts upon humans that they like in a seemingly generous manner, but these gifts usually come with some kind of catch.

A wise Monster Hunter avoids the Fair Folk at all costs.

I do not recommend Hunting Fairies. I strongly suggest giving them a wide berth whenever possible. However, since it is not uncommon for Monster Hunters to come across the Fair Folk in our travels, it is best to know how to defend against them.

Fairy sightings happen most often at noon, midnight, and twilight. They can occur anytime in the year, but the chances are best on May Day, Midsummer's Night, and All Hallows' Eve. They tend to collect in forests and other spots in nature, away from cities and human construction.

There are some advanced spells that will give you Fairy sight so you can see through their invisible cloaking or their glamours, but the most effective method is a Fairy ointment applied to the eyes.[13] According to legend simply carrying a four leaf clover is said to reveal the Fair Folk, though I am skeptical of this belief. Children can also see Fairies at times because they retain the innocence of youth, but I don't recommend bringing a child in contact with Fairies as kidnapping is always a possibility even in later childhood.

Humans are woefully outmatched when compared to the magic of the Faerie Realm, but we are not entirely defenseless. Iron is like poison to Fairies. It will not kill them, but it will weaken them immensely. Not just iron weaponry, but any iron in the vicinity, including that used in construction. This is the main reason it is safer to be in modern cities as the Fey do shy away from them. This is also the reason Fairies have upset construction plans as well. They enjoy playing on the Earth and anything that inhibits that is seen as an attack.

Other items known to repel Fairies include salt, St. John's Wort, flax seed on the floor[14], and the sound of bells. Some recommend sleeping with a knife under the pillow, which I consider sound advice in most situations. Mind you, one must take care with this practice as I have had more than one apprentice lose an ear in the middle of a particularly fitful sleep.

---

13.   Be cautious. If a Fairy catches you using Fairy ointment, you will be punished.
14.   Fairies are easily obsessed with picking up every seed.

Fairy Folk

Pixie (or Pisky): This tiny creature is only a few inches tall and is responsible for our most common image of Fairies. It usually dresses in green and wears pointed hats, but it does not have visible wings. The Pixie is a mischievous creature that likes to mislead travelers and make off with horses in the night, riding them to exhaustion.

Dwarf: Compact and powerfully built, the Dwarf reaches full maturity in only a few years. It primarily works as a miner, digging for gold and other precious treasures and is a skilled metalworker. It cannot venture aboveground during the day or it will turn to stone.

Goblin: The Goblin is among of the most evil type of Fairy and easily the ugliest of the Fair Folk. It is roughly a foot tall, but can alter its size and shape, growing to large proportions or taking on the form of animals if it chooses.

Brownie: A roughly three-foot tall, friendly house spirit that completes unfinished chores in the nighttime. In exchange, the brownie expects to receive small tokens of appreciation. If these gifts are not given, the Brownie will undo all the work it has done and leave your home in worse shape then when it started.

The end is just the beginning...

Monster Hunters will continue the fight against things that go bump in the night for as long as there is evil in the world. Whether it is a sentient malevolence that plots and schemes or an animalistic urge that simply feeds its hunger on human flesh, we will take it on and we will conquer it. Failure is never an option.

Take what you have read in these pages and apply it in your training. By now you should have a better understanding of Monster Hunting and whether or not it is your calling. Not everyone can accept this challenge. Not everyone should.

Don't think that these words alone will prepare you to face down a Demon or battle a Werewolf. There is a long road of training ahead. Seek out more experienced Hunters. Ask them to teach you their craft. It is only through the community of Hunters that we will one day prove victorious.

My instruction may end here, but my stories will not. I will continue to share my tales with you in other formats to give you a better idea of what the life of a Monster Hunter entails. It is my hope that the knowledge I provide will help us all one day win the fight and allow all Monster Hunters to retire in peace and with most of their limbs intact.

About the author

John Paul Russ is an expert survivalist and monster hunter. He began hunting vampires as a teenager alongside his father, John Russ Sr., and has since fought, captured or killed a multitude of creatures and cryptids over the past eighteen years. Russ has hunted hundreds of different monsters from Zombies and Werewolves to Bigfoot and the Loch Ness Monster and he is one of the most well regarded experts in his field.

Russ currently resides in the state of Pennsylvania and has no immediate family to speak of aside from his Labrador Retriever, Zeus, who accompanies him on many of his missions. A documentary about Russ' life and exploits begins filming in 2012.